WOW, GOD

WOW, GOD

Sister Francis Clare, S.S.N.D.

P.O. BOX 311, GREEN FOREST, AR 72638

Dedicated to two of the greatest Charismatics of all time, Francis and Clare of the 12th century, and to all of God's people whom I have come to know as my sister and my brother.

I wish to express appreciation to Frances and Charles Hunter for first encouraging me to write; to Mother Georgianne, my Provincial team, Sister Mary Julia, Sister Regina Ecker, and Sister Joseph Marie who have been most helpful in encouraging, supporting, and discerning my growing and my writing; to Ann Aiola, Becky Dudley, Marcie Donelan, Eileen Connolly, and others for the typing; to St. Raphael's Prayer Group, Father Joel, and Father Donnolly for reading and discerning; and most of all to my publisher, Cliff Dudley for the hours spent discerning, refining, and recapturing with me the purpose and the story that is *WOW GOD.*

First Printing 1975
Fifth Printing 1980
Tenth Printing 1982
Fifteenth Printing 1988
Sixteenth Printing 1990

Library of Congress Catalog Card Number: 75-32009
ISBN: 0-89221-131-8

Cover design: Darrell Wiskur
Back cover photo credit: Walter Robb

CONTENTS

FOREWORD

All around us are signs that God is renewing His Church, and His people. One of those signs is the Charismatic renewal. Through it millions of people have come to believe and really experience that God, the Father of the Lord Jesus Christ, is our loving Father. He loves us. He loves me! Through it they have come to know Jesus Christ as Lord and Brother. Through it their lives have been opened to the gift and the power of the Holy Spirit.

Sister Francis Clare shares her experiences in this book. The value of any literary work is gauged by the test of time. With this printing comes my blessing on a book that has touched me deeply and appears to be anointed and a powerful witness to the goodness of God among us.

Whether man approves or disapproves, blesses or withholds blessings, is not the issue. What is the issue, I think is whether or not people's hearts are touched, lives are changed and God is glorified in the process. For all for whom this is happening I pray: "May the blessing of the Lord be upon you!"

Most Reverend Raymond A. Lucker
Bishop of New Ulm, Minnesota

PREFACE

And I, if I be lifted up, I will draw all things to Myself.
Jesus, I lift You up as author of this book that You may draw
to Yourself all to whom I reach out in love as I begin this
writing.

You have a story to tell. And I'd like to sit back and let
You tell it . . . like it is.

This is the story of my rediscovering Fire. Of Your rescu-
ing one little nun on the way out of religious life after
twenty-five years of being in. It is the story of the old
gospel lived, the full gospel believed, and the new
Pentecost happening, not just in my life but in lives all
over the world.

It is another twentieth-century love story in which I
have learned that to love is to say I am sorry and I forgive,
beginning with myself.

From the start it has seemed strange to have a title
clearly given before I had anything to go with it. *Wow,
God!* came to me one day during a teaching on praise; it
was given as the American idiom for the Hebrew word
Hallelujah. The title is a combination of *Hallelu*, meaning
"Wow," and *jah*, the shortened form for Yahweh.

God, I praise You for every *wow* way You have worked
and will work in the lives of all who will read this book.

It is no accident that you are together here. There is a big gap between charismatic religious and non-charismatic religious in many communities . . . you cannot bridge that gap . . . I have brought you here to bring you closer to Me . . . In proportion as you die to yourself and learn to rely solely on Me, I will bring about unity in your communities. You will have much to suffer, but you can depend on My strength . . . They will see your weaknesses and say, "This must truly be the work of God."

Chapter One
Ready to Quit

"I was one of those nuns on the way out of religious life when . . ."

Thus I began my first testimony at a Wednesday evening service in a little Assembly of God church down the street from our convent on Mulberry Street. I was not the speaker that night. I had hoped to slip in *in cognito* to hear Lloyd Dugger, former television country-western star with the Red Foley Ozarks, now turned minister.

Mingling with people of other faiths was not something new to me. For the past four years I had been an active member of an Ecumenical group of teachers from Mankato (Minnesota) State College. Each couple was of a different denomination, and so our monthly meetings were sparked with dialogue. We ran the gamut of our differences and our likenesses—Lutherans, Presbyterians, Methodists, Congregationalists, Baptists, Quakers, Catholics, and atheists.

But this was different. To dialogue was one thing; to be at a prayer service with people I had known only to joke about as "Holy Rollers" was another thing One part of me was very much at home, for the people gathered were friendly, warm, outgoing. The other part was alive with contradiction, tradition, prejudice. An inner voice within me said, "Run!"

Somehow I found that I couldn't run; something within me had just stopped running. I had just discovered both the What and the Who I had been running from—and it wasn't the "Holy Rollers."

All my life I could have cared less if they were holy or if they were rollers. Now as I saw them kneel in prayer, enter into a spirit of worship, and lead the congregation in song, I knew there was something holy about the people, about the place, and about the God they were worshiping.

I didn't want to run. I didn't even want to walk. I just wanted to stand, worshiping the living God in the songs they were singing: "O Magnify the Name of the Lord," "There's a Sweet, Sweet Spirit in this Place," "From Glory to Glory He's Changing Me."

Here was something beyond the Living Room Dialogues of the past four years. Here was the Spirit of the Living God "ecumenizing" His people in the songs we were singing, in a common experience of the Holy Spirit released in our lives. As I listened, I was moved with the realization that God was doing something.

I was just beginning to feel really at home with what I was seeing, hearing, and feeling when Rev. Anderson startled me with "We are really pleased to have with us this evening a Catholic Sister who has just received the Baptism of the Holy Spirit. Sister Francis Clare, would you like to give a testimony?"

At that time, "testimony" was so foreign to my Catholic ears that my first inclination was to dig into my purse for whatever the Reverend was calling for.

As a matter of fact, I did not want to give a testimony. But I rose to my feet in spite of myself, and in one sweeping statement gave my State of the Union address: "I was one of those nuns on the way out of religious life when this baptism of the Holy Spirit empowered me to stay."

After I sat down, it surprised me not a little to think that I had declared so definitely a truth that I had not even shared with my Sisters in the convent down the street.

That was in the fall of 1969; I had been baptized in the Holy Spirit at the conclusion of an interfaith charismatic weekend.

That was the last thing in the world I wanted to have happen to me. I knew a few people who were "that way," and they did not do a thing for me except turn me off and generate new currents of unbelief.

When the *National Catholic Reporter* flared those first headlines in the summer of 1967 about people "having a good time praying together," my thought was, *Forget it.*

My mind was open about being closed. My simple judgment was, people who believe like that, pray like that, and gather like that are much too far out for me. What I didn't know then was that sometimes you can be so far out that you are in.

At that time I considered my stand in a changing church certainly not that of a deadly conservative—hardly that of a middle-of-the-road person. Quite proudly I considered myself vigorously *avant garde.* I was a Teilhard de Chardin nut, reading everything I could get my hands on, absorbing Teilhard tapes like a sponge, and traveling long distances to hear de Chardin lectures. *The Phenomenon of Man,* and *The Divine Milieu* were the about-to-be-fulfilled Books of Revelation for me. They held the explanation of the past, the wonder of the present, and the promise of the future.

Not only was de Chardin a favorite, but I subscribed enthusiastically to all that modern theologians were writing, thinking, and encouraging.

11

You were really "in" if you could theologize, philosophize, and scripturalize about what these men were saying. There were days when this kind of sharing not only built us up, but completely drained all our individual and corporate energies.

We'd enjoy a lull. Then some new controversial article, provoking book, or stirring author would break the doldrums, renew our vision, our hope, and our certainty that there would be a brand new day for all of us—for the whole church, when enough of God's people absorbed enough of these revitalized truths.

So I thought, So we thought. So others thought.

We were keenly aware of a spiritual knowledge explosion that warmed, expanded, sometimes all but "blew our minds." But if we were looking to this to do a work of renewal, renewal wasn't happening.

What was happening was a swinging open of some of those "windows and doors" Pope John XXIII was calling for. What was happening was a clearing of horizons, an adjusting of rear-view vision, and a rearranging of priorities. A resurrected people were encouraged to rise to their feet in worship, to clap their hands, and to strum their guitars.

As if this were not enough, books, weekends, and sensitivity sessions explored the psyche, the subconscious, the inner needs of an I-Thou relationship. They challenged in us the apathetic, the bored, the dislocated, the questioning, the feelingless, to a holding and shaking of hands and a sharing of an ever-deepening awareness of the God-sized vacuum within us. They kept us searching, always hoping to find; reading, always hopeful to discover; looking often to dried-up cisterns for that Living Water.

It was this spiritual knowledge explosion that finally brought me to the end of my road. And I found myself in the fall of 1969 asking to walk a new road, that of exclaustration—living outside the cloister, not dispensed from my Religious Vows but walking in obedience to my Bishop rather than Religious Superiors. I would have the privilege of returning after one year to be reinstated as a School Sister of Notre Dame.

I never did take that road, for I discovered another, the road of a Spirit-filled nun. Robert Frost's poem describes my dilemma and my choice:

"Two roads converged in a wood . . .
I chose the one less travelled by
And that has made all the difference."

I have loved you with an everlasting love. My affection for you is constant. Sometimes your love for Me fades; sometimes your love for Me is doubtful. My love for you is not that way. My love for you is constant. Even when you are asleep I am loving you. I am loving you from all eternity with a love that is infinite — a love that is without measure. I am always mightily in love with you, infinitely in love with you.

My daughter, come to Me. I want you to see My face. Look to Me. I am your God. I am your Lord. I am your Savior. I am your Spouse. I have called you. I have called you by name even from your mother's womb. Even before that I can say that in My Father's womb you were called. You were called from all eternity to be My special one.

Chapter Two
Bits From Way Back

I can't remember a time when I did not know about God. In my earliest memories God was there, as Someone I had been taught to believe in, as I believed in Santa Claus, fairies, and the boogeyman. Only it seemed to me that God was much more real, for He was not only Someone I could learn to love but Someone I could hurt.

I learned to pray at my ma's knee and on my pa's lap. Long before I went to school I can remember our family of nine kneeling, leaning on the kitchen chairs, as we prayed our after-supper devotions. No matter who our company was, they were invited to join.

Prayer was the heartbeat of our home, pulsing through times of joy, sorrow, and need. Living on a farm was living close to God and He was always there to ask or thank. If a storm threatened the crops, we lit the blessed candle, and prayed until the sky cleared. If the horses, cows, pigs, or chickens took sick, we might pray first and get the vet later. When the chicken thieves threatened in the night, Pa would get the shotgun, but Ma's ammunition was her rosary beads.

Even before I knew what it was all about, worship was always something I almost instinctively wanted to be part of. I have memories of a particular Sunday when I ran crying after the car because I was told that I could not go along to the Sunday Mass. As a family, we weathered every kind of hardship to be in our place at the Sunday worship. In spring we plunged through the mud with the horses and wagon. In winter we plowed through three- and four-foot high snowdrifts on sideroads and in fields with horses and sleigh just to be at Mass.

Our family was quite a religious family by all the standards of the 1920s and 1930s. If there is such a thing as a traditional family, we were that for generations back.

Reading the Bible is something that people of all denominations closely associate with loyalty to their faith. While Bible reading was not discouraged in our family, it was not formally encouraged, despite the fact that Pope Leo XIII as early as 1900 wrote an encyclical encouraging the faithful to read the Scriptures. And Pope Pius X wrote: "To be ignorant of the Scripture is to be ignorant of Jesus Christ."

Neither ma nor pa were Bible-reading Christians, but they were Ten Commandment and Seven Sacrament good Catholics. We loved God, loved our neighbors, and loved ourselves.

Our Bible was a family heritage for recording family records of marriages, births, important family events, our family tree, and deaths. As part of our family library it was used on occasion for research. Never do I recall anyone just sitting down to read it because of fashion or need.

I possessed an insatiable appetite to read everything I could get my hands on. Rarely was I given the job of dusting our living room, for invariably I would start and end with the bookcase or the magazine rack. I recall setting the table for dinner one evening with a stack of dishes in one hand and a book in the other. Yet I have no recollection of ever flipping the cover of our family Bible to see whether it might have something interesting or challenging for me to read.

The Bible was something we listened to the priest read at the Sunday Mass. It was something we later read stories about in Bible History. And on the college scene we took courses in Bible so we could say, "I read the Good Book."

Never was it the first book to be picked up in the morning and the last laid down at night. I never felt the need to have one that was my personal possession. In my Novitiate I gave away one that had been given to me as a personal gift.

Now wherever I go, my Bible goes with me. My first criterion for a new purse is, will it hold my *Living Bible*. For extended stays my suitcase always carries my *Jerusalem Bible*. In the past one was too many—now two is too few.

I see now that my parents' lives were a living Bible with a lot of the idiom, grip, and directness of the Taylor paraphrase. Ma and Pa were religious people with a First Commandment heart, a Baltimore Catechism mind, and calloused Catholic knees.

I came by it naturally—drinking in the love of God with ma's milk, pa's discipline, and grandma's cookies. "Praise the Lord" was widely used in my grandma's house. Our greeting on meeting, going to bed, and rising in the morning was the German "Gelobt sei Jesus Christus" (Praise be Jesus Christ). To which the other would answer, "In evigkeit. Amen" (Now and forever).

The world beyond was never far out of reach for me. I recall that Grandpa Schares died when I was five. Because he had always been a gold mine for pennies for my piggy bank, I was concerned when the supply was cut off. "Grandma," I asked, "where is Grandpa?" "He's in Heaven," was her reply. "Where's that, where's that?" I pleaded. "Way up in the sky, honey!" For hours I waited, looking at the "way up there," expecting Grandpa to let those pennies fall from heaven.

I was a child of strong impressions and active imagination, for I recall one day they told me there was another place "way out there" for bad people and there was a fire there. One night on seeing a fiery sunset, I was sure this was the "way out there" hell and that the fire was showing through.

Often today I am both amused and amazed at the gross inaccuracies of my knowing and coming to know something of the veiled mysteries of God. Grandma Mangrich used to tell about the day of my first Communion at the age of six when I ran into her arms after the service exclaiming, "Oh, I am so happy! Grandma, I'm so happy, Jesus came into my heart today."

From the very start there was in me the combination of the saint and the sinner. In preparing for my first reception of the Sacrament of Penance at the age of six, I set out to memorize the entire list of possible sins for a child—thinking that to have a really good confession I would have at least one of each. As I was talking in my sleep one night Grandma heard me sailing down the whole litany of sins I was preparing to confess. With much love and tender care she set me straight.

Born January 25, 1925, I was taken to the village church just five days later to be baptized Alma Rose. With my Uncle Peter Winniger and Aunt Rose Even acting as godparents, Father Mayer performed the Ceremony of Baptism consisting of an entrance to the Church, the exorcism of any unclean spirit, the anointing with oil, and the pouring of water. My godparents spoke for me the profession of faith and the renouncing of Satan which I renewed for myself at the time of my First Communion. At that time I received again the white garment and the burning light given as symbols of my "new life" — my being "born again."

Today the wisdom of infant baptism and early Communion is often seriously questioned both by theologians and parents. I can only say that I have pleasant memories and a sense of growing with much gentleness into a strong mature experience. If I had not had the grace of these early sacraments, there is no telling how much less real God might have been to me. I can only know that with them, I knew God's presence, His saving power, and His love.

Living on a farm the first thirteen years of my life had its mixed blessings. With the plenty of opportunities for creating adventure there were also plenty of jobs. Even though there were nine of us, we all had our duties at various stages of growth. There was a sense of growing importance when we outgrew one job and grew into another. Filling the woodbox and a basket of corncobs for burning in the kitchen stove was the first. There were a lot of carrying and fetching jobs: water from the windmill, butter and milk from the cooling tank, bacon and ham from the smokehouse, radishes from the garden, and apples from the orchard. Gathering eggs was something I was trusted with on occasion, but milking cows was one feat I tried but never fully mastered. Many times I would have preferred milking cows to doing supper dishes, but with five brothers and one tomboy sister, my performance was considered slow, second rate, and unprofessional.

I had as much dare in me as anyone, for I can remember scaling the heights of a windmill, the barn lofts, and thirty-foot ladders. Only once do I recall a fall and broken bones. With two big orchards there were always trees we were allowed to eat from and trees with forbidden fruit. One day we discovered a way to get around a command not to pick the fruit of a particular tree. Within reach of our mouths hung the most delicious apples, and with a little bit of luck, we managed to eat the apples right off the tree, letting the cores hang as testimony of our heroic obedience.

My five brothers, three sisters, and I were all disciplined from an early age by both ma and pa. Every Christmas Krisskind would leave a small bundle of willow sticks beside our other gifts for anyone who had need of them in the coming months. This was not something we feared a lot, but we all knew that if we had it coming, it came.

For the most part my relationships with my brothers and sisters were normal. Together we had some of the best little league softball, football, rollerskating, ice skating, sleighing, and home entertainment. When we fought about work, Ma used to say, "You really ought to fight about doing the most, for then when you get to heaven you'll have much more piled up to your credit." I guess we all had some of the old "works" theology.

The most distasteful thing about being the youngest of four girls was getting all the "hand-me-downs." The best thing about being the "baby girl" was getting out of things for the same reason.

In contrast to the modern ungraded classrooms that many of our Catholic schools now boast, I spent my first eight years in two-grade classrooms. They were good years. I loved school, loved learning, loved the kids, and loved my teachers.

In the winter of my eighth grade Ma suddenly became very ill. The diagnosis was a cancerous tumor of the stomach for which even the doctors had no hope. They could not remove it without danger of Ma's bleeding to death. Every traditional prayer, offering, and shrine possibility was exploited but to no avail. We sought out friends with bottles of miraculous Lourdes water, miraculous medals, and novenas that never fail. But they were all failing us.

I locked myself in my room one day—praying, bargaining, and promising: "God, I will even go to the convent, if Ma would only live." Already at that time in the back of my mind I was thinking about some day becoming a nun. I kept the thought, the daydream, and sometimes the nightmare, way back in my mind, for it seemed such a preposterous thing to even think about doing. Nuns were such out-of-this-world people, and I really loved being in-this-world.

Sometime during my eighth grade year, I received in the mail a booklet entitled: *Shall I Be a School Sister of Notre Dame?* My first reaction was a combination of anger and fear, that someone besides myself should know that I was even thinking about "shall I." My second thought was more practical—a decision to bury the book rather than read it, for fear in reading I might discover that I should be a Sister and then I would have no excuse for not being one.

In the spring of that year, one Sunday morning while all the family was at Mass, Ma died —— quietly, beautifully, unexpectedly, but prepared.

I can still recall one of my first thoughts after the first realization of loss. "Okay, God, if that is the way You want it, I won't go to the convent. If you don't care enough about me to answer my prayer, I've had it! You had better know I'm not going to be one of Your nuns. Now or ever! Do you hear me? Not ever!"

If you go searching about within yourselves for your own talents to use, you will find them worthless.

You too are part of My treasure. Sometimes I give you to others but remember that you belong to Me. You are part of My treasure. Could there be greater happiness? Think of what it means to be My treasure. Could anything be compared with that? Does it not mean that you are very dear to Me and does a man not protect His treasure? I mean to protect you. I mean to polish you and to keep you bright. And the cloth that I will use to polish you is love. And if it rubs hard at times, remember it is love held by a loving hand.

Chapter Three
The Academy

What happens to a young girl, what happens to a father, what happens to a whole family when the strongest bond that had held them together is severed? Pa suffered the most. Yet as far as I know he never shared with any of us. Ma's death was something we never mentioned. We really did not know how to handle the hurt in ourselves or how to help the hurt in the other. What had been our home became just a house we came back to when nothing else was going on. I was still angry with God because of Ma's death, but I couldn't resist the pull to convent life. I was tired of the whole mess. I wanted to escape from the hurt and pain of the house without Ma.

Sensing this as well as a definite call to be a Sister, I welcomed the chance, though I was just thirteen, to go away to boarding school. Good Counsel Academy, about two hundred miles north, seemed the ideal place to begin my high school and my aspirancy to be a nun. This simply meant that besides my regular high school program I joined an Aspirancy program with a group of girls who felt an early call to religious life. We were given special training in the spiritual life, in meditating, and in discovering what it might mean to become a nun after we graduated from the Academy.

I had a lot of religious relatives. One of Pa's five sisters became a School Sister of Notre Dame, and four of Ma's eight sisters joined the same order. All of them had a great interest in my future education and a feeling that some day I would be joining them. Perhaps it was in answer to their prayers that the way cleared and stayed cleared. If prayer got me to boarding school, it took more prayer to keep me there.

During my four years at the Academy, I was as happy and carefree as anyone once I mastered the loneliness of never getting a letter or a visit from my ma. During the first year I often cried myself to sleep with loneliness. I would find myself asking God, "Why, why, didn't you hear my prayers? Why, why, did you have to take my ma?" I would fight back the sorrow and the bitterness, for that could never be part of the new life I was to have as a nun.

Making friends was a challenge—never a problem. School activities could really excite me, drive me, and inspire me to any goal. Lives of great people had me reading like mad. Dreams of great people had me dreaming. The holiness of saints had me wanting to be like them. I became a member of the Hall of Fame of the Alpha Beta Tau Society. This meant that for four years I rated with the top fifteen at the Academy in knowledge of my Catholic faith.

Knowing about God was one thing; getting to know Jesus was another. And getting to know the demands He can make on your life was still another. There were many times when the spirit of the world, my own fleshy vanity, and a growing love for the things of the world got in the way.

More and more I realized the pull away and I'd catch myself running from what I had known. Through it all, there was always that Voice, like a bursting sea, a booming

24

cannon, a gentle breeze, or a golden thread coming through in the most unexpected places and at the most unpredictable times.

As high school kids we plotted one day to have a party with an All-Saints theme. Someone made up nonsense verses for our guests to draw. The slip I drew struck with the realness of a prophetic word at a prayer meeting: "A saint you are called to be, but oh, just yet there isn't any show." I read and reread the two-line jingle. There really wasn't any show. If anything, there was a show of the opposite.

"You going to the convent! That's a laugh, why you run around a lot more than I do," my sister Mary challenged one day during summer vacation.

Thinking about it, I replied: "It's not enough just to say that you have a vocation. You have to really test it." What I didn't know then is that you can make the test so rigorous that you don't pass it.

I really loved the fun and the things of the world, and I was happiest when lost in a world of fun. Because Ma was no longer there to moderate, Pa gave me a great deal of freedom. I could go where I pleased, when I pleased, and as much as I pleased. And I pleased a lot. Pa never really minded as long as the kids were "good."

By the time I reached the summer of my junior year, as certain as I was that I had had a religious vocation, now I was sure that I did not have one. There were too many other things to do with one's life. That was the summer I fell both in and out of love. In, because he was really a nice kid. Out, because I knew that nothing short of completely belonging to God would give me the happiness I was looking for.

"Vanity of vanities and all is vanity, save to love God and serve Him alone." Much of my senior year was punctuated with this cry of Solomon. I would go out, have the best time imaginable, come home and realize the bubble burst. Nothing remained but a burning realization that all the good times in the world could never fill me. They could only leave me more empty.

"Too many dances. Does life hold nothing else worthwhile?" was all my aspirant's directress wrote from St. Louis.

In me there was much of the Dr. Jekyll and Mr. Hyde, of the old Eve and the new Mary.

Until the night of my departure it was an interior battle. I wanted so much for someone in authority to say I did not have a calling so that I would not have to give up everything. But no one in authority said it.

There were others who questioned but they did not matter. I recall the last shopping trip before I entered the convent. I was shopping for the kind of black granny shoes Sisters wore at that time. The young man waiting on me asked "It isn't really any of my business, but why are you buying this kind of shoe?"

"Oh, I am entering the convent in a few days," I said very matter-of-factly. It always made such good sense in telling it to someone else.

"My, but you are young to be disappointed in love," was all he said. Really perplexed, he packaged the granny shoes, and I left very much amused. The more I thought about it, the more amused I became. Then not only was I amused, but I was inspired with the real truth—not disappointed in love, but appointed to love. Jesus' love.

I will teach you from day to day. You have so many things to learn but a lifetime to learn them. Listen to My voice. There will be sunny days and cloudy days. The way will be smooth and rough. There will be many paths you will want to take. But let your fascination be only on Me. Remember I am your strength. I am food for your journey. I will be your sun and your gentle rain. Look to Me. Am I not a God of Love?

What sorrow cannot love overcome?
What adversity can it not bridge?
What mountain can it not climb?
What depths can it not leap over?
Love and My love will give you wings.

Chapter Four
The "Jump In"

From the outside looking in, locking oneself behind convent walls may seem to be the folly of follies. I remember the night before I leapt not out but in. I was afraid until my cousin, Father Frenchy, who was having dinner at our house advised, "Jump in. Once you are in the water is fine."

That gave me courage and proved to be good advice. It was about a two-hundred-mile jump north. Once there, the water was fine. Not only the water but everything about the place—the Sisters and the crowd of twenty-two who entered with me. They were great women. Many had everything in life. But they knew they wanted to give that everything to God despite obstacles from within and opposition from without. Some were old friends from boarding school, one was an R.N., a few had been working for several years, and a few had been handpicked from the prairies of North Dakota.

Together we had some of the greatest growth times. Living in the convent is not at all like *The Nun's Story.* Sometimes my students used to say, "Sister, what is religious life like? What is it like when you are not teaching our classes? We read *The Nun's Story* (or we saw the movie) and it seemed pretty awful."

And I would say, "Fellows, I've read the book, I've seen the movie, and I've lived the life. And it is not like that. Anyway in my experience."

Being a nun can be a beautiful, joyful, and fulfilling life. From my first years in religious life I experienced all of that. I loved Jesus as any young bride loves her husband, and I knew His love for me.

A Novitiate year is not meant to be an easy year. It is meant to be a year of testing. We were completely cut off from any visitors, family, or friends,—receiving or sending letters was limited to once a month. We were set to learn the cost of discipleship as a School Sister of Notre Dame—to discover the beauty and the price of belonging to Jesus in a life of vowed gospel poverty, dedicated celibacy, and obedience. For me it was a year of examination, self-searching, and hunting for God.

As I left the Novitiate my directress, Sister Mary Julia, handed me a card on which she had written: "I have found Him whom my soul loves. I have held Him and I will not let Him go." The words I recognized as Solomon's Song of Songs. The truth I recognized as my life. I knew I had found Him whom my soul loves. I knew I would never let Him go.

Mission life was my first real testing ground. Assigned to Wabasha, a little town on the banks of the Mississippi, I grew to love the people, the work, the teaching. Some of the early castles crumbled, and new ones needed to be built. I learned to bend my will and adjust my vision to another's insight and discernment. Many of the days were beautiful and filled with the fruit of the Spirit. Others were the hard living out of what we had learned in the Novitiate. I came to know the truth of "To live in heaven with Saints is bliss and glory. But to live on earth with them is quite another story."

"Be a good Sister!"

"Keep the Rule and the Rule will keep you" was a maxim we learned in Novitiate days.

The Rule for rising was up at the crack of dawn . . . seven o'clock was sleeping late. Tradition taught us to respond to the rising bell with this prayer: "I will arise and put on Jesus Christ the Crucified whom my soul loves and in whom my heart rejoices."

Each part of our holy habit was put on with a prayer. At the veil we prayed, "Lord, hide me in Your heart and in Your sacred wounds. I desire not to see the things of the world nor to be seen by the world."

"May my tongue cleave to my mouth if I do not remember thee," was a prayer we breathed as we entered the convent parlor to visit our family several times a year if they were close enough to visit.

The Great Silence was a rule every good religious kept from night prayer at seven or eight until after breakfast the next morning. In my early years in the convent all our meals with rare exceptions such as Christmas, Easter, and Pentecost were taken in silence while one of the Sisters read from a spiritual book. The purpose was to feed our souls and spirits even as our bodies were fed. (Today the discipline of Silence is left to each Sister's discretion.)

There was a lot of routine as well as challenge in running a good classroom. Creativity and discipline were set up as twin goals. Some Sisters were naturals at both.

For me creativity was a natural; discipline was a supernatural. I found myself praying, consulting, and practicing what I might do about some of the problem children. In order to keep a straight face when correcting one particular class I engaged myself practicing model sentences I might use on the culprits.

Like a general in *The Charge of the Light Brigade,* I learned to wield Tennyson's: "[Yours] not to reason why,

[Yours] but to do [or] die."

All said, discipline was neither my greatest virtue nor the lack of it my greatest weakness.

Midway I aimed to enjoy my years of teaching. Sometimes students had quite a unique way of showing their appreciation. On the closing day of school one sixth grader presented me with a sympathy card reading: "May our dear Lord and His Mother console you in your great loss . . . of us" they added, and signed their names. I don't know how any teacher can survive without a sense of humor.

"Dem Bones" was a religious play I used to love producing with students during Vocation Week. The plot explained the three bones necessary for a religious vocation—a prayer bone, a backbone, and a funny bone.

I believe God gifted me with all three. One day a student thought to startle me by putting a dead mouse on my desk.

"Too bad it's dead. It would be a lot more exciting if it were alive," was all I found myself saying.

There was many a situation when only humor saved the day. After a long, detailed explanation of a new learning program, I paused intending to sit for a moment. Instead I tipped off my swivel chair and was pinned under the desk. Three layers deep—starched nun, swivel chair, wooden desk. I couldn't move so I called forth the order: "You've got to get me out of here."

Six valiant students immediately engineered the rescue operation: first the wooden desk off—then the swivel chair off—then the starched nun up! No bones broken, no pain anywhere. Time for a good laugh!

Snap! went the rubber band. Down the aisle rolled a sea of oranges and one lemon.

My mouth hung open not in hunger but in wonder. "This sixth grade! What next!"

Class officers leaped forward, gathered up the "juiced

32

up" oranges and presented them as a gift. "Orange juice for you, Sister."

"Hi," I said to two little fellows sitting in front of a drug store on the streets of Minneapolis one day. (I was dressed in Habit No. 1.)

"I ain't never seen anyone dressed like you before," the littlest guy said as he clung to his five-year-old brother.

"I did," the older brother consoled. "When I went to kindergarten there was a lady dressed like that."

"But you don't wear those clothes all the time," the three-year-old challenged me.

Before I could answer the five-year-old spoke for me. "No, she's got clothes at home just like our mother has. Haven't you?"

"Not really. I like these better so I wear them all the time," I settled.

It took a little minute for that to sink with the littlest guy. Then he piped up, "But you don't have to wear underwear with all those clothes."

Before I could defend myself his brother chided, "You shouldn't ask such questions!" My street car came; my day was saved.

I guess we presented a pretty scary picture to a lot of little folk. On coming home around dusk on Halloween, two of our Sisters met two little guys going out for "tricks or treats." A quick look and then a quick question, "Hey, did you scare anybody yet?"

To be creative and to show initiative you tried the untried. One time I remember setting up a Student Appreciation Week during which I wrote a special note of appreciation for each of my forty students. Years later I was amazed to receive a letter with the return address of a federal correctional institution in Iowa.

"Dear Sister Francis Clare," the note read, "A lot has happened since I was in your sixth grade. While serving a term here in prison I asked my mother to bring me some of the things I saved over the years. Mom brought me the note you once wrote telling me what you appreciated about me. Even tho I've gone bad—perhaps you can still think of something nice to say about me. If you can—write to . . ."

It was the summer of 1949. I was working toward finishing my degree in English and history at St. Catherine's College in St. Paul. The day before the Fourth of July, word came to me that my youngest brother, Gene, whom I had not seen for five years, was drowned on a Sunday afternoon outing. Just seven when my ma died, he was now eighteen and out of high school one year.

The fact of the long separation from Gene together with the strictness of the Notre Dame Rule at this time increased the pain of loss immensely. We were not permitted to go home for the funeral of a brother or a sister because of the strictness of our enclosure. We were permitted only two home visits in a lifetime—one for one's mother and one for one's father. One could choose to take it when they were living or at the time of their death.

The feeling of loneliness and bitterness once again gripped me. Bitterness mixed with pain, Gene was gone. "God," I cried, "why? What are you trying to teach me? First my ma! Now Gene! How can I continue to live when You keep killing me with these deaths?" Again there was silence.

Not permitted to go home for the funeral, I experienced the ultimate of what the death of a loved one can mean. There was no measuring, no describing, no real sharing the depths of my pain.

A "coincidence" was a real source of consolation to me

34

during my time of sorrow. At the very hour when Gene was drowning, as I was in prayer in our convent chapel, I suddenly had the thought to pray for someone who would meet with sudden death over the holidays. That thought had been with me all day. But just at four o'clock, at the hour of Gene's death, I was saying to God that if there was anyone on our family tree, God should apply these prayers for that relative in need. Everyone who knew Gene knew that he was prepared to go whenever God might call.

Sometime before Gene's death, in a moment of poetic fancy, I sent home this bit of a parody for our family as it was in the winter of 1948:

Eleven happy people in the Schares family when
Mom left for heaven; then there were ten.

Ten saddened people left to mourn and to pine,
An Irishman got Addie; then there were nine.

Nine the population for to cook and to bake,
Ray found a wife, and then there were eight.

Eight lovely people could still be a bit of heaven,
But Mary married Orville; and then there were seven.

Seven friendly people fully alive and with tricks,
Laurie married Bud, and then there were six.

Six hardy people can surely survive,
Yours truly joined the convent; and then there were
five.

Five reunited people; the boys were back from war,
Leo married Eileen, and then there were four.

Four precious people were all you could see,
Vince met JoAnn, and then there were three.

Three wonderful people just a little bit blue,
Al became Celeste's and then there were two.

Two lonely people, just father and son,
God keep them together, never let there be one.

It was like a bit of prophecy now finding fulfillment, for just two months after Gene's death, I was summoned home at the sudden death of my pa. I don't know how I managed to rise above so much sorrow in so short a time except that even as I sensed my sisters' husbands were a great source of strength and comfort to them—even so Jesus was for me.

One day someone thinking to empathize with me offered: "Jesus must love you very much to give you all that suffering."

"I wouldn't mind if He didn't love me quite so much," was all I could respond.

I turned to and found much comfort and a kinship of spirit in the philosophers and the poets. These words from Aeschylus capsuled strength and a sustaining power for me: "In our sleep, pain that cannot forget falls drop by drop upon the heart and in our despair, against our will, comes wisdom through the awful grace of God."

During the time of my formation in the Novitiate, we were not encouraged to have close friends with whom we could share the secrets of our inner being and our spiritual walk. And so the comfort and help that today might come from a particular friend was markedly absent at this time in my life.

Six years after my temporary profession as a Sister, I

prepared to make my commitment for life. During the time of special preparation never once did I question whether I wanted to make Final Vows nor did I question if I had a calling to be a Sister. I knew it was a tough life as well as a beautiful one. And I knew I wanted to live it.

My challenge was to seek out all the high-powered ways I could discover in the summer of 1951 to really live it up. I resolved to meditate the full life of Jesus every day while praying the fifteen decades of the rosary. My thought was to fill my day so full that I would have no time left to wonder, worry, or fret. I just wanted to give 100 percent of my life to Jesus, not just 99.5 percent. My last eight days before the ceremony of Final Vows were spent in a complete silent Jesuit retreat. God had every chance to get me and to take from me everything that was not of Himself.

Ever since my freshman year in boarding school, I had the habit of stopping by a favorite statue in the chapel at Good Counsel just to think things through and to talk things over. Mary had always been someone special, especially after Ma's death. A person, a presence, a power I could turn to. "Son, behold your mother," was a Scripture that spoke to me; "Mother, behold your son," was a Scripture that held a promise for me. What Mary was for Jesus, she could be for me. And so as I stopped by on the night before my Final Vows, I turned my thoughts first to Jesus saying, "I really want to give You my whole life. One hundred percent forever! But I am such an Indian-giver. You know how I keep taking back the minutes, the hours, the days . . ."

Then I prayed, "Mother, I ask you to take my life and give it to Jesus, give Him the whole package and see that I neither keep back nor take back the least bit of it." It was just a passing thought from a heart that had known this Mother's love.

Suddenly it was as if the heavens opened and the power

of God poured over me like a tangible sheet of peace and presence. It seemed every chain that had ever shackled me fell right there. Joy unspeakable began to well up inside of me, and I was literally bathed in the glory of God for I don't know how long. I only know that when I got to my room that night I experienced a new love from God I had never known.

The next day when I got up I was like Moses come down from the mountain. I almost had to hide my face. I remember the Sisters remarking: "What happened to Francis Clare? She's really turned on."

And I was, in ways I could not explain. I could only experience for the next twenty years. I didn't know what had happened to me. All I knew was that I had experienced Jesus in a new way. I was so conscious of Jesus in me and Jesus in other people, that I discovered myself feeling and doing things that I knew were purely Jesus acting in me and through me.

For the first time in my life meditation was a breeze. I could read a sentence and meditate an hour. I had never been able to do that. A short time before in making a fifteen-minute meditation I might check my watch five times to see if the time was up.

Television came out a short time after this, not just for people in the world but for those of us who had separated ourselves from the world. Sisters were beginning to get excited about the "boob tube" and the few good programs we could see right in the convent without going out. Somehow I could never get excited because I knew that I had "an inborn set." I could open the Scriptures and that was my television screen. I saw hour after hour of living color. It was like someone had thrown a power switch and I was both seeing and experiencing the Bible for the first time.

I still did not know what was really happening. I did not know why I had to stay awake at night to praise the Lord by the hour. I did not know why I could not sleep at night because I experienced so much of God's love. I tried at times to explain these times to my Spiritual Director or to Retreat Masters as I thought I was responsible for holding on to and building on to these experiences. The most I could get from priests was, "Be a good nun." And the most I could get from God was, "Be still and know that I am God."

While I was in the Novitiate I had read a book about a nun from Germany who discovered she could not pray to the Holy Spirit any more because she was so full of Him. Next she sensed the Presence of Jesus so completely that she was one with Him. Then she completely identified with the Father. Then she died, all within a year. I thought, "Oh, I'm not going to live very long. I'd better get that book and read up on what I should do next."

Back to the Novitiate I went and discovered the blue book entitled *Life of Light*. I thought I was going to read it. But the Lord put His hands on mine and said: "Be still and know that I am God. You're not going to have to do it. Let Me do what I want with your life."

For the next twenty years, in much light and some darkness I went on, not knowing what this experience was. Only that it was real . . . and that it filled me with a hope, love, and joy that nothing could dampen or lessen. I remember that when I was working for my master's degree at Loras one of the guys challenged: "Sister, sit down here. I have to find out what makes you so damn happy."

My daughters, Psalm 65 is no accident. This Psalm is to direct you in the way I want you to live. I want you to sing My praises; I want you to live in My joy. I want you to feed on My pastures. I want you to be the water that helps to quench the parched souls of men and women. I want you to let people drink of My Spirit through you. Through you there will be new life, through you seeds will sprout. Through you seeds will bear fruit, and will blossom forth to the honor and glory of My Father. I want you to use it as a way of life. You're to sing My joys, you're not to wait on the world; you're to get started. You're to be a barometer of Christian life by the way you portray joy. Joy is to be your way of life.

Chapter Five
God, I Want It

For almost twenty years I bugged a lot of people because I was so "damn happy." Often during this time I wondered how I had ever lived before I knew this peace, this joy, this power, this Presence. I wondered how other people lived without whatever this was.

Occasionally during this time I would come across someone who had had a similar experience which they could not explain either, but in which they found abounding joy and amazing grace. It was more than just belonging to the Pepsi generation or knowing the reality of a new stress on the Resurrection.

It was as if I had a whole new set of inner dynamics to comprehend the films I saw, the books I read, the courses I took, and the classes I taught. There was a power to sift, to sort, to see beyond. In dealing with people there was a power to see beyond what was happening as on a spiritual television screen.

Looking back now, I realize that a lot of what happened in my teaching of religion was a release of anointed teaching to meet people's needs.

Long after the Bishop had been around for the ceremony, I made a special practice of having the students renew their Confirmation graces. It just seemed right to pray daily for the release of the seven gifts in our lives: the wisdom, the understanding, the counsel, the fortitude, the piety, and the fear of the Lord.

Having a minor in history, one of my favorite amusements has been to discover how history repeats itself. And yet I never dreamt that the "Upper Room" repeating itself would be the thing that would completely change my life at forty-five.

In the days of all the "starch and serge" there were many moments of the good, the true, the beautiful, and the charming in my life as a School Sister of Notre Dame. Our habit had always been considered one of the most artistically beautiful with a perfect balance of the black and the white, the pleat and the fold. According to tradition it was a habit designed in heaven. On Christmas night of 1597 the mother of Jesus is said to have appeared to our French foundress, Blessed Alix LeClerc, dressed in our religious habit. Holding the Christ Child in her arms, she offered Him to Alix with the words: "Take this Child and make Him grow."

For hundreds of years, thousands upon thousands of School Sisters of Notre Dame have accepted this challenge, worn this habit, and dedicated their lives to making Him grow in the hearts of millions of youth around the world.

Many Sisters can recall awesome and humorous incidents connected with being that special kind of person framed in that special habit, pedestaled by both parents and children. One of the more humorous and stirring for me was the time about fifteen years ago when I was walking down a school corridor past a line-up of about fifty pre schoolers about to register for the first grade. With an awe that shone from his eyes and was betrayed in his voice, one of the little fellows piped up as I passed, "Hello, Mrs. God!"

We don't hear things like that any more.

What we do hear in the very depths of our being as we delve through the Living Word is God speaking to us in tones that call all His people to be that bride of Christ, that is, "Mrs. God." Through the prophet Hosea we are called to be His faithful bride: "Come, let us return to the Lord; it is he who has torn us—he will heal us. He has wounded—he will bind us up" (Hosea 6:1, TLB).

It was the fall of 1969, when I came into what might be called a vocational crisis. In late August I had returned to my convent home on Mulberry Street after spending ten weeks teaching for the government in a CHOICE Program at Fort Valley State College in Fort Valley, Georgia. It had been a good summer, but a hard one with long hours of exhausting service. The blacks there were a beautiful people, and the team I worked with knew dedication. I loved sharing my life with them. With the help of closed circuit TV and video tapes we brought "the King's good English" to bridge an area of need between high school and college.

I loved counseling the youth, and I did a lot of thinking that summer about what their problems really were and what the answers were not.

Old problems haunted me for new answers and I knew that they were not in theology, in philosophy, or in the Scriptures as I knew them. Here I was with a people not just different because they were Georgian or black, but different because they knew little or nothing about the Christianity I professed to be the answer.

The more I reflected on the lives of students I had known, the lives of Sisters, and my own life, the more I doubted that Christianity as I knew it was the answer. There had to be more.

I thought back on the little hotbed of Christians who had been nurtured in our grade and high school for the past twelve years, and I was faced with the truth in my perception—they were not so "hot." What is "hot" about Catholics who without force do not go to church on Sunday, do not receive the Sacraments once a year, and will argue away the binding morality of the Commandments of God and the precepts of the Church? As I looked at the collected fruit of our dedicated lives in our students, I saw more and more clearly that whatever we were doing, the fruit just wasn't there.

With this crisis in thought came a crisis in seeing purpose in the lives of the people I lived with—in seeing meaning in my own life. Religious life became very, very empty, very, very blah! It was like someone had "blown" it. What I didn't know was that the Holy Spirit was about to "blow" it.

Religious life became for me like the albatross from "The Rime of the Ancient Mariner." In my dilemma, I searched the old books again, but I got no new answers, only more questions. I talked to people. It was as if we had parted company. I attended the most promising lectures and conferences, braved encounter weekends, held hands in sensitivity sessions—all I came home knowing was that I had a problem. I was empty with a God-sized vacuum, broken like a Humpty Dumpty, seeking . . . .

If I had not had all the training I had in guidance and counseling, I might have thought that I needed to see a psychologist or a psychiatrist. I knew that I did not have that kind of problem. Still, I could not explain why all of a sudden, after twenty-five years of happiness as a religious, life was suddenly darkness as I had never known, emptiness as I had never suffered.

One day in late September, while walking this labyrinth, I sought out Mother Margareta, Provincial leader for our Northwest Province, to share my utter frustration and the decision to leave the convent for a year. "I don't know what has happened to me. It is like the bottom has fallen out of my religious life," I told her.

"But Sister, you've always been so happy in religious life," she said.

"Yes, I know. But I am not now. I can't stand nuns any more. They bug me to no end. The only way I can do justice to the way I feel is to leave the convent for a year. Away from here surely the pieces will come back together, but not here."

With this Mother Margareta offered, "I'll pray for you."

My thought was, *A lot of good that will do.* But I promised to stick it out until Christmas.

One day in the middle of October when I was thoroughly bored with living, I decided to take in a CCD (Confraternity of Christian Doctrine Convention) in Minneapolis. Looking over the list of speakers, I could not find one I was even slightly interested in. For the sake of the intellectual game, and I really set out to play it like a game, I decided to take in this talk on Catholic Pentecostals.

Not because I thought they had any answers; in fact, I was sure they did not have any for me. It was my intent to sit back while they were speaking, all the while loading my barrels, preparing to shoot holes through everything they said.

After the talk I sat back as the rest went up to say their pretty little things—to ask a question, to share some similar experience.

Then it was my turn. I remember glorying in my remarks. "There is no way any or all of this makes sense! It sounds pretty, but you can't expect me to believe it. God isn't that way. I can't believe that the kind of things you were talking about can really happen. And even if they could, don't expect me to believe them!"

After fifteen minutes of negative response, Judy Norris and Sister Justin realized that I was really turned off. In fact, Sister reported to me weeks later that Judy had finally turned to her and asked, "Who was that nun who was so turned off?"

I went home that night with copies of *The Cross and the Switchblade* and *They Speak With Other Tongues,* for Judy said, "Sister, we can't answer your questions, but maybe these books will." To be polite I accepted the books all the while thinking, "If I really get hard up some day, I'll read them. But don't expect it."

The books sat on the shelf for about three weeks. Finally one night I had reached a new low in boredom—bored with living, bored with people, bored with problems, bored with no answers, and bored with a God who seemed more dead than alive. I really felt heavy, weighted like Atlas with the world on my shoulders.

In desperation I reached for *The Cross and the Switchblade,* and began to read. The more I read the more curious I got. This man was talking about a place where I had traveled the previous summer after my return from Georgia. I knew the highways and the byways that Wilkerson was talking about. I could identify those streets, those kids, those problems.

I found Dave Wilkerson's words quite unbelievable, yet absolutely fascinating and shockingly true. No way could I put that book down. Neither could I realize what was happening to me until I had raced halfway through the book.

Suddenly I was furious. Here was this gangster, this Nicky Cruz, this guy who had broken all fifteen of the Ten Commandments, in a relationship closer to God than I was. He knew God in a way that I didn't. He experienced the power and the love of God in his life in a way that I sorely lacked.

I cried out to God, "This isn't fair. Here I have been a

nun for twenty-five years, and whatever You've done for Nicky Cruz, You've never done for me!"

I was the elder son in the Gospel's parable of the Prodigal. I wept. I prayed. I read some more. I read to the end of the book in one sitting.

When I got to the place where Wilkerson explains the baptism in the Holy Spirit, I checked the copyright date and questioned, "God, how can this be? This isn't for today, or is it? This is the twentieth century; You can't be pouring out your Spirit again like in the first? Or can You?"

Gradually the truth dawned, and I saw Dave Wilkerson in a new light. I saw him with a courage that warmed, with a love that caught, with a power I sorely needed. I saw Nicky Cruz in a new light, and I was glad that he was the younger and I the elder son.

Somehow like the Gospel parable, the Father does have the whole of an inheritance for the elder son too . . . when he gets spunky enough to say, "I want it."

I prayed, "Father, I want it. I want what that gangster's got."

Look, My daughter, look at Who it is who is leading you. Look at Who it is who is calling you. It is I Myself, the Lord God and Savior, the One Who redeemed you and the One Who is your God; the One who is your everything. Look to Me and you will have no fears. Look to Me, I am the Savior of all. I have called you by name. And you know that you can hear Me when you listen. Listen carefully and you will hear Me and I will call you not only by name, but I will call you to where I want you to go. I will tell you which way to go. You will only need to look and listen and you will be able to follow.

Chapter Six
This Was That

Finished with *The Cross and the Switchblade,* I delved right into *They Speak with Other Tongues.* All the while I kept checking for documentation. I was impressed. A kaleidoscope of questions started flashing.

What if I were prayed for? What if I got what he got? What if I didn't? If this were real, what was I going to do about it? If it wasn't, and I got hooked, my last state could be worse than the first. Sister Mary had warned me, "Fran, you may be in a bad state, but don't worsen it with this Pentecostal thing. And if you do, don't say I didn't warn you."

There was no clear path either "in" or "out." I had never heard of nuns in a convent praying in tongues. Yet, if this were real, what better place? We had just given up praying in Latin . . . now to take on tongues? I was repelled; I was attracted. I saw light; I experienced even greater darkness. I groped for peace, but confusion threatened. I needed answers. My head dizzied with questions. If I came "in" this could really lead me "out."

Jerked about by my indecision and limited vision, I finally found myself attending my first inter-faith charismatic prayer meeting. About thirty people of all religious backgrounds gathered in one of our Academy parlors for their usual meeting. What was usual for them was very unusual for me. They turned me both on and off.

They turned me on because they were real, warm, and genuine. But they turned me off because it was strange to hear everyone praying at the same time in phrases I had never been part of. "Amen! Hallelujah! Glory to God! Praise the Lord— Glory to You, Jesus!" mingled with the sound of other tongues. I found it hard to get used to this kind of "freedom in worship."

I wasn't sure that I wanted to. Like Tevye in *Fiddler on the Roof* I kept going back and forth from the one hand to the other hand of tradition. On the one hand I liked the still kind of worship with people listening to each other. On the other hand, there was something to be said for this new experience of worship, this sense of power, this beauty of tone, and the feel of "Holy, Holy, Holy." On the one hand, I liked the casual, natural, down-to-earth pose of prayer. But on the other hand there was something to be said about this freedom of lifting your hands in worship to praise the Lord.

What I didn't know then was that God was simply saying, "Stick 'em up! Surrender!"

But I couldn't. A couple of weeks later an inter-faith charismatic weekend was at our Newman Center, given by a Lutheran, a Baptist, and a Catholic priest. The first night of the retreat there was a film depicting people from all over the world seeking as never before a greater union with God. I thought, I can buy that.

Later in the evening during a mini-prayer meeting I heard for the first time the prophetic gift of tongues. I thought, Weirdo! I can't buy that!

Then I remembered that, in a sense, we had been singing in tongues for years. We really did not know what we were singing when we sang songs like "Tantum ergo sacramen-

50

tum." We just knew that we were praising God.

I went home with mixed feelings: feelings of desire, feelings of fear. "God," I prayed, "I'm not going back. I'm not going back unless You speak to me about it and speak clearly."

At that time I didn't know that people "cut the Book." I borrowed a Jerusalem Bible (Can you imagine, me a sister for twenty-five years and I didn't own a Bible), cutting it for a message, and reading from Luke: "Stay in Jerusalem until you are endued from on High" (24:29).

"Lord, You do speak clearly!" was all I could say. Then I added in my own defense, "But I am still scared to death of whatever this baptism is."

The next day I went back. The fear lifted as I heard others tell of the same fears in their searching for and running from the baptism of the Holy Spirit. The Lutheran pastor, Don Photenhauer, shared his experience of the ongoing revelation—his seeing, his backing away, his seeing some more, backing some more. Finally when he could no longer deny the light, he opened the door to experience as never before the glory of the heavenly courts and the fiery trails of the earthly courts.

In an attempt to play the Good Samaritan to neighbors who had been robbed, stripped, and left by the wayside praying in tongues, the Baptist preacher thought, "I've got to go to the Nordby home and help these good Lutherans out." Instead they helped him "in" . . . and he got the baptism.

Listening, I realized that each of them, even Father McCarthy, had this same donkey approach that I was experiencing. It was one step forward and two backwards. You see a little. You back away. You see a little more. You back away some more. You catch the whole vision and you come to realize that this is *what you want, what you need.*

51

As the retreat team shared the effects of the gifts and the fruits released in their lives, the lights began to go on. They shared how the Scriptures really came alive, how the incredible love and presence of God came into awareness, how the desire to praise penetrated their days and more and more of their nights, how the chains of the past suddenly fell away, how their lives were dramatically changed overnight.

The more they shared, the more things opened up and the past added up. "And I never knew what it was," I gasped.

That night before I took my Final Vows . . . that experience I had of a mighty outpouring of light, grace, and glory . . . that feeling that had left me so "happy" . . . that incredible walk in light, love, presence, and power prior to the dark night. Could it be? It must be! This was that!

Sometimes from My vantage point it's funny to see you struggling. It's funny to see your worries. My Father in heaven laughs at your little efforts, laughs at how hard you try. All you need to do, My daughters — this is the secret — is to rest in Me. All you need to do is to open up to Me. All you need do is to remember the cloud is opening up right over you, standing there being baptized by My Holy Spirit constantly.

Chapter Seven
Baptism of Fire

"Anyone desiring the baptism in the Holy Spirit tonight, go to the little chapel." I didn't need a second invitation. I didn't need anyone to decipher what I really had or what I still needed.

I just knew that if there was something more God was offering, I wanted everything I could get. If you needed to be hungry, I was hungry. If you needed to be thirsty, I was thirsty. If you needed to be broken, empty, and desiring to be filled, I was broken, empty, and desiring to be filled.

Because I wanted to prove further to myself that I believed Jesus was the Baptizer and that it didn't matter who prayed with whom, I deliberately sought out the Lutheran pastor for prayer. Before Don prayed he asked, "Sister, what would you like?"

I didn't know that you asked for anything more than that Jesus be your Baptizer, that He fully release within you the fullness of His Spirit.

I had a happy thought; "I would like to receive this baptism of the Holy Spirit with the same disposition that the mother of Jesus had while she waited in the Upper Room. I want to receive with her faith, her trust, her desire, her love."

"I don't understand," Don said.

"I know you don't. But I do, so let's have it that way."

I got it that way. As Don prayed a peace poured over me that was so real, so profound, so complete, that the next day I could not recognize my human anatomy. It was as if I had a whole new cell arrangement. The albatross of the last three months was gone. The cloud that had held me in darkness was lifted. I knew only light—joy—Presence!

The Lord spoke through Isaiah 60:1-3 and 20-22:

"Arise, shine; for your light has come, and the glory of the Lord has risen upon you. For behold, darkness will cover the earth, and deep darkness the peoples; but the Lord will rise upon you, and His glory will appear upon you. And nations will come to your light, and kings to the brightness of your rising . . . . Your sun will set no more, neither will your moon wane; for you will have the Lord for an everlasting light, and the days of your mourning will be finished. Then all your people will be righteous; they will possess the land forever, the branch of My planting, the work of My hands, that I may be glorified. The smallest one will become a clan, and the least one a mighty nation. I, the Lord, will hasten it in its time."

As I walked into my bedroom that night, it was as if someone had passed away. I had the sense of walking in light, of being a new creation, of needing to clean up on the old. Jesus had broken the fetters, created a presence, released a "dam."

The next day I started cleaning up. I got rid of all that savored of search and bondage! Books, papers, writings, things! All of this had never given me the peace I had sought. I came across a beautiful printing by Teilhard de Chardin, philosopher, scientist, theologian: "When man has mastered the winds and the waves and has harnessed for God the energies of love, he will have rediscovered fire."

In Jesus, in the Word, in the new Pentecost, I had rediscovered "Fire."

In the clean-up, I got to a Christmas card that I had designed. It was something I was really proud of, for it was a clever combination of pictures from my summer in Georgia and New York. It was my social gospel way of saying Merry Christmas. You know the thought—if you can really "hang in there" with the poorest of the poor, if you are willing to share their life, then you are really living religion.

Jesus wasn't on that card but people were. People who had a need. It seemed to me that my medium was my message—the real message of Christmas—"people who love people."

I found the Lord saying, "Throw it."

I was quick to argue, "But Lord, You can't mean it. This is the cleverest, most meaningful card I have ever designed. It is only three weeks until Christmas. I don't have time to design another."

The Lord came back, "Throw it."

I took it with me down to the burner But when I got there I chickened. "Lord, You ask too much. This time I can't."

I took it back upstairs to my room. Two days later I tried putting on the final touches before the printer would do his job. It now seemed to belong to someone else. There was no way I could relate to that card. I surrendered. "Okay, Lord. You can have it. But You are going to have to give me something in its place. And I'm not going to have a thing to do with it." As I walked out of my room the first person I met was the art teacher. "Sister Pat," I asked, "Would you letter something for me on a Christmas card?"

"Sure. What?"

Without thinking I found myself saying: "Praise the Lord for His Pentecostal birth in '69."

Then I panicked. "Oh no, God! I can't do that." It is one thing to have an experience, it is another to tell the world. What will people think? A Catholic nun turned Pentecostal! My mind was deluged with reasonable objections. Suddenly I could care less what people thought—if this was what God was asking, then it must be done.

Since then it has become more and more easy to be willing to "tell it on the mountain" that I am "that way," that I believe that way, that I walk that way. For me there is just one way: Jesus, and to be filled with Him, His love, His Spirit, His gifts, His power, and His praises!

"If anyone publicly acknowledges me as his friend, I will openly acknowledge him as my friend before my father in heaven" (Matthew 10:32, TLB). I don't want to miss out on that promise.

If there is one thing that I have learned, it is that we do not make a mistake in following those quiet inspirations of the Spirit. I received more responses from those Christmas cards with a short testimony inside than from anything I've ever sent out. And not people saying: "Watch it"; "Cool it"; "Come off it."

Instead they demanded, "I've got to hear more about this experience."

Using all my resources, I sent out more copies of *The Cross and the Switchblade, They Speak with Other Tongues,* and *Catholic Pentecostals.* As the Spirit moved I met a need in Georgia, New York, California, Arizona, Kansas, Iowa, and even Rome. In sending copies to my friend, Sister

Kathryn, in the Generalate in Rome, it was my hope that Mother Georgianne, Mother General of some ten thousand Notre Dames, would take to reading them.

Later I heard from Sister Kathryn that the day after they arrived, Mother Georgianne had asked, "Does anyone know were I can find a copy of *Catholic Pentecostals, The Cross and the Switchblade,* and *They Speak in Other Tongues?* I've sent downtown in Rome three times to get them but there seems to be no place where we can buy them."

Urged by Sisters in the States, Mother began reading the books with great interest and openness. Several months later I had an opportunity to share some of my experience with her. I can still remember Mother's quiet amazement as she said, "Sister, do you realize that you are the first live Pentecostal I have ever spoken to?"

I am your world of Joy. Anything else is sham and will not last. Do not seek comfort from anyone else but Me. Do you not think I am capable of giving it?

Am I not the treasurer of good things? And have I not opened the door for you? And have I not invited you in? I do not mean that you should only look. I mean those treasures to be yours – to have and to be used. Do not seek treasure elsewhere. You will only find false gold and it will become tarnished and bitter.

I let you know your weakness sometimes so that you may know where your treasure really lies.

Chapter Eight
The New Nun

I had crossed my Rubicon, there was no going back. Nor did I want to. More and more I began to sense that my whole life was changed.

The dark night was day, the restless stilled, the empty filled, the chained set free. Things I loved I could hate, people I hated I could love, and where I was powerless I knew power.

"Stay in Jerusalem until you are endued with power from on high" was the promise. I had stayed and I was endued.

On leaving the classroom the Wednesday before, I had known that I just wanted to throw in the towel on my life as a nun and as a teacher. On returning the following Monday I was a new creature facing a new scene. It was a brand new day. It was an entirely new ball game—with outs canceled, strikes deleted, opponents defeated, and a whole new team playing. I never felt so certain that I was playing on the winning side.

Even the posters on the classroom walls flashed a new message. One in particular—a huge close-up of Martin Luther King—had a few small words down in the right hand lower corner which I had never noticed before. Now they shouted at me: "*He that is not willing to lay down his life for a cause is not worthy to live.*"

I knew that whatever this fire was burning within me, I had to be willing to lay down my life to spread it across the face of the earth, the face of my classroom, the face of my convent, the face of my family.

I remembered Jesus saying, "I have come to cast fire upon the earth; and how I wish it were already kindled" (Luke 12:49). Having experienced the fire, I knew I needed to dare the casting and the kindling. I had never felt so fired to go.

Yet like Isaiah, I knew that God was not just in the fire, or just in the earthquake, but for me, a beginner, He was most surely in the still small voice. So I began to listen as never before.

As I listened I experienced a honeymoon of basking in God's love, exploding with His praises, and realizing, with little effort on my part, the gifts and the fruit of His Spirit.

I had been to my doctor a few weeks before for my annual checkup, and since he did not find anything wrong, I suggested to him that he might give me some tranquilizers to bridge the times when both the nuns and the students got on my nerves. I returned to witness that I had found the Tranquilizer.

My personal relationship with Jesus Christ had come alive again with new dimensions, extending into the moments of every day, every relationship with others, every searching out of the Scripture. In a short time it became evident to many that I had changed. The change was evident to Mother Magareta, for I was no longer asking to leave the convent. Instead I was asking to use my Christmas gift money to attend the January Charismatic Leader's Convention in Ann Arbor, Michigan.

"You don't have to tell me. I can see it. You are really changed." Mother not only allowed the trip, but paid my way.

The change was evident to my principal at Loyola High, for when someone asked Father Ben's opinion of the Pentecostal experience he was quoted: "I don't know much about it from reading, but one thing I can say, Sister Francis Clare is an entirely different person since she has had the experience."

I praised God when I heard that for I had not shared that much with Father Ben. Fruit can speak louder than words.

As time went on Loyola became more and more alive for me as a place where God had been working, was working, and would work a new thing. I saw much need, much hunger, and a limited openness to this new Pentecost. Knowing how long it had taken me to catch the light, to understand the working, and to set my feet on the path, I knew that I needed to have infinite patience for God's timing with others. I knew that I couldn't do a lot of explaining of what I was just beginning to understand myself.

And yet as my own Humpty Dumpty was coming together again, I could see more and more clearly that Jesus was not only the answer to every problem in my life but that Jesus was the only answer in the lives of my students. I became alerted to opportunities to share what I had discovered. One day I invited Ken, a Spirit-filled senior in Business at Mankato State College, to share in one of my classes.

"You know," Ken shared, "my mother had a Bible in our home for twenty-seven years, but never once was I even tempted to flip the lid to see if it might have anything in it for me. The night I accepted Jesus Christ in my life as my personal Savior, the Bible came alive for me. When I got home I began to read. I read and read and I read. The more I read, the more I discovered that there is no personal problem I will ever have in my life that Jesus is not the answer for. Nor is there any problem the whole of humanity will ever be asked to face but that the answer is right in that Book."

Credibility grew as more doors opened. I found it good to be brave about asking people to share at our Loyola assemblies—people I would never have dreamed of asking before. Jim was one of those gang guys who if Jesus had not gotten him the law would have. Bill had a hair-raising, hell-bound story of being rescued from an O.D. of drugs to know a B.A. (Born Again) life of glory.

God can use all kinds of people to bring all kinds of people to a full-blown experience of Himself. And yet we so often mistrust His choice of instruments. Because of where we were, because of where our students were, and because of where these Jesus People were, there was some mistrust about the whole happening. I was asked to warn Jim and Bill: "It's all right for you to tell of your experience of getting straight with the law and coming off drugs, but I've been asked to ask you to leave Jesus and religion out. We're not ready for that."

But Jesus was ready and so as the front door closed He slipped in the back. After their sharing at the school assembly Jim and Bill invited to Laughlins anyone who wanted to hear more about how Jesus had helped them.

Five students not only accepted this invitation but later that evening they accepted Jesus' invitation: "Behold I stand at the door and knock; If anyone hears My voice and opens the door, I will come in . . ." (Revelation 3:20).

Besides teaching English, I was assigned to several counseling periods a day. I recall, when this first happened, I tested our principal out with: "Are you remembering that I am a Pentecostal? I may be tempted to use some of that kind of power."

Father Ben replied, "Use any kind of power you have for any kind of problem we have."

This was quite a challenge. A lot of things happened that year.

God began to show us that often in a counseling situation we are dealing with not so much a student with a problem as with a person being controlled in an area of his mind or emotions by principalities and powers. So the thing to do in an area where a student is spinning wheels is not to spin wheels with him but to remember the power we have. "These signs will accompany those who believe . . ."(Mark 16:17).

As I began to believe, I began to see the signs following. As students came to me with their areas of difficulty, I never once hinted that I would take authority of an evil spirit or cast out a devil. That might have "scared the devil out of them." Accepting them where they were and bringing them where the Lord wanted proved to be the path of wisdom. It seemed imprudent to analyze their problems for them as an area of spiritual bondage. So I simply responded to their need with, "Would you like me to pray about that?"

Sometimes I would add, "If you don't mind, I would prefer to pray in another language. It is easier for me that way." There are times when explanations only confuse. (I suppose many of them thought it was just a nun praying in Latin.)

The important thing was, it worked. I remember the first time I sat back to praise God for a marvel just done.

Deeply distressed and complaining about her migraine headaches, a beautiful young girl came to me seeking what I might do. I didn't know a thing I could do . . . but I knew what God could do. I remembered reading that migraine could be a spirit. "Would you like some prayer?" I asked. As I prayed in my spirit, I took authority of the spirit of migraine.

Two weeks later she was back. "You know, Sister, I haven't had a headache since. But I've got these other problems I would like you to pray about. I get so jealous of my boyfriend every time he looks at someone else, or someone looks at him, that it is ruining our relationship. I can't stand my parents. I'm filled with resentment, hatred, and rebellion. Several times I've attempted suicide . . ."

One after the other my mind registered the spirits to be dealt with: the Hate, the Rebellion, the Depression, the Jealousy, the Anger, the Suicide. I knew that Jesus had already won the victory over all of these and it was just a matter of claiming it. We prayed, believing.

Several weeks later she was back with the good news. "I haven't had trouble in one of these areas since." It was good news based on that other Good News: "He anointed Me to preach the gospel to the poor . . . to proclaim release to the captives . . . to set free those who are downtrodden .

I am a Rogerian-trained counselor: trained to listen, reflect, reassure, wait for long-range solutions, trained to have your client discover the answer to his own problem, trained to pray *about* problem students but never *with* them. Discovering this was like suddenly acquiring another Master's Degree in counseling. The first still serves as excellent background but the second is definitely the most excellent foreground.

It's amazing how many times this power of the Spirit can be applied not just to individuals with a problem, but to the broader school scene. I seldom entered a classroom where I thought there was going to be rebellion, hatred, and resentment coming from the world outside, that I did not take authority over the forces of evil before I entered. What a difference when I forgot.

Today, instead of fighting people, we are often called upon to resist the principalities and powers that might be controlling them. We don't fight the devil. Scripture says; "Resist the devil and he will flee from you" (James 4:7).

What is true for the individual can be true for the whole school assembly.

One day after the senior leaders had been threatening a heaven-knows-what assembly around the time of the Kent State University troubles, Father Ben challenged Sister Ethel and me as we were leaving school that day: "You'd better get that Holy Spirit working."

My first thought was, A fine thing to bring Him in for emergency. How about having Him here all the time?

The second was more in line with Holy Spirit thinking. It led the two of us back to a classroom to pray.

After suggesting that Sister might pray over me in proxy for the assembly, first I caught, then I cast out, *fear.* The Lord gave us a Scripture that reassured: "Fear not . . ." As Sister prayed she took authority over the spirits of rebellion, hate, fear, confusion, mockery, tension, violence, pride and others that might have controlled the students that last day in the assembly. We prayed for about an hour, as the Lord gave us to pray. Then we just knew it was finished. And it was.

The following day Loyola had the most peaceful assembly we had ever witnessed—an assembly in which students dealt with students, listened to students, questioned students with the amazing consideration, courtesy, and thoughtfulness. The powers that had held them in bondage were bound at least for that assembly. The result was that no one insisted on the big street demonstration. The students were awed with what had taken place, and only Sister Ethel and I knew the secret.

As time went on, it took more and more discipline for me to maintain a balanced enthusiasm for the old passion of teaching English and literature. Now teaching was definitely in second place; Jesus was in first.

This didn't put good teaching out; I did some of the best innovative teaching I had ever done that year, especially in poetry. Both the students and my enthusiasm for a finished project on poetry urged me to write and publish my first article "Poetry Teach-ins—An In Thing." I had never had that kind of ambition before.

Jesus was yet another way to discover life and what living is all about. I couldn't say a lot because I was not teaching Religion, but I could always challenge my literature students with a statement or a question.

Occasionally I heard little rumors that some parents were disturbed because that "Pentecostal Sister" was talking about Jesus in her literature class. With the principal and our school philosophy to back me I had little fear of the student or parent critic. I could always reason and rationalize: "Literature is life; so we need to be open to the whole of life—not just the good, the true, the beautiful, the heavily polluted, and the strangely plotted, but the abundant life long ignored and denied."

Occasionally both in and out of class some student might confront me with a line such as: "I can't believe it. God isn't alive like that, doing things like that. This is the twentieth century." And I would think, "Words right out of my mouth just a few months ago."

It's a strange thing even with my family. Here I had been a religious for twenty-five years and suddenly my family became disturbed because I turned "religious." I began talking about Jesus as if I knew Him. I began to talk about the Bible as if I believed it. I suddenly identified with the power to do as He did . . . to reach out in compassion to free the suffering, to lay my hands on the sick, to take authority on evil spirits, to pray as if I expected God to meet the need right now.

For some He did. The pain in that back, that migraine headache, those varicose veins were gone. Together we discovered—Jesus Christ is the same yesterday, today and forever.

Whenever you see streams, think of My love working its way throughout the land . . . bringing refreshment to all it touches. You will be those streams. You will bring refreshment. Remember the Water in the streams is Me. You are but the channels, the riverbed through which I can run. Remember it is the water that directs where the channel goes.

And it is by the power of the water that the riverbed is made. The riverbed of itself does not say, "I will go here or there." It is directed by the power of the water. Do not let the water become polluted. If you allow the full force of the water to go through you, the water will stay pure. It will sparkle; it will sing; it will be a thing of beauty, joy, and refreshment. It will bring forth fruit and flowers.

See that you put nothing to dam up the water because then the water will become polluted and be of no purpose. If you but knew the force of My Water. Its full force. It will push away all obstacles.

Chapter Nine
North Carolina, Here I Come

Someone has said that before you have a charismatic group pray for you, you had better be sure that you want what you are asking for.

I wanted what I was asking for—direction for some summer work, hopefully interracial with some Pentecostal dimension. In February I placed my name to serve again in the CHOICE program. In March I placed my petition before our prayer group.

A lot of doors began opening and closing. The end of May came and there was just one door still open: a possibility for ten weeks of teaching and counseling in Long Island, New York. There was no witness within me either to teach that long or that far away. So I sought discernment from one of the leaders in our prayer group.

Butch shared with me that several months before when we had prayed for my direction he had seen two lines of light come down and one of them went way out East. I thought, "Hmmm, that means that I should consider Long Island."

Quickly I wrote and quickly they wrote back saying, "Sorry, we changed our course to philosophy."

"The lines didn't mean anything anyway," I mused.

May ended. The middle of June came. Five days before A & T State University opened its doors for their summer session, I received a long distance call from Chicago Headquarters. "Sister, would you consider teaching two summer courses: "Introduction to Guidance" and "Introduction to Counseling?"

A litany of "buts" immediately sputtered forth: "But we just buried my sister, and I had thought to help the family. But I had a real desire to attend my first International Catholic Charismatic Convention in June. But there was also an invitation to attend the Full Gospel Businessmens' Convention in July. I am awfully sorry, but . . . some other time."

After I hung up, I suddenly remembered those lines of light. "Lord, did they mean anything?" I panicked.

Not waiting for a reply, I opened the Scripture to James 1:5: "But if any of you lacks wisdom, let him ask of God, who gives to all men generously and without reproach, and it will be given to him."

"Lord, I am asking," was all I said.

"Sister, I am giving," was all I heard.

Boldly I phoned back. "I am not saying yes or no, but I will say maybe. You do realize I am not prepared?" I shied. "I should have five weeks—five months—and you are not even giving me five days . . ."

"You can set it up any way you want, when you get here. I have great confidence in Sister's teaching . . ." the admission director assured me.

"But I really feel the Lord wants me to grow in the knowledge and experience of the Charismatic this summer. There is this conference at Notre Dame . . ."

"No problem. We will see that you get there."

With instant boldness I found myself saying, "But there is this other conference in Chicago the whole first week in July . . ."

72

"No problem. We will see that you get there and substitute your teaching."

It was getting unbelievably ridiculous. God was knocking down all the barriers and supplying all the means.

I weakened. "Nothing but the grace of God could make me come."

"I am content with that," Mr. Armstrong said.

Besides the Gospel "staff and sandals," I left Minnesota with thirty copies of *The Cross and the Switchblade* for giveaways.

Finally in Greensboro, there was just time enough to discover the Shertzer and Stone texts and the course outlines. Before I fell into bed that night I fell to my knees praying, "God, You got me into this. Now how are You going to get me out of it? What do I do with these blacks? They are different. I just cannot go in there like a white do-gooder . . ."

"Give them a copy of *The Cross and the Switchblade.*"

I said, "God, You have got to be kidding!"

"Trust Me!"

I trusted. And it didn't take them long to understand that in a lot of cases we are facing not just kids with problems, but kids ruled by principalities and powers. These counselors had been on the school scene and they knew the kind of hopelessness that can reign on both sides of the desk when the most you can say is, "I understand that you have a problem."

Free to tell it like it is, I shared from Notre Dame and from Chicago things relevant and faith-building. About midway through the term the men began asking, "Sister, we would like this baptism of the Holy Spirit."

"I'll take you to the Full Gospel Businessmen," was all I could promise. At that time I had never prayed with anyone for receiving the baptism. What if I prayed and nothing happened?

The next Friday, there was a dinner meeting at which I had been asked to share with Doug and Dixie Raye. Both classes were invited to be guests of the businessmen. For both the black and the white, there was never a night like that night.

Coming to class the next day one of the men remarked, "Sistah, that was the first time we was in a white society where there wasn't a phoney in the bunch."

What was happening in our classes had an overflow in the lounge among the professors. "Sistah, I've been looking for that all my life.When will you pray with me for the baptism?" a doctor of philosophy challenged.

We prayed on Friday. On Monday I greeted: "Doctor, how is it?"

"Sistah, I'm still sizzlin'." He went on to relate how he was in a state of perpetual amazement the whole weekend; how the pieces of his life seemed to be falling together and arranging themselves in a whole new mosaic.

While at the Chicago Hilton I rode the elevator one day with Pate Boyd and his wife from Greensboro, North Carolina. Pate was God's choice to introduce me to the Catholic circles as well as Protestant prayer groups.

The first night I attended one of the home prayer meetings, Pate tipped me off. "People have been meeting in the Mason home for over twenty years, but never has there been a Catholic, much less a Catholic nun attending. You may expect anything from old Grandma Mason."

The warning was well-grounded for there was a dubious warmth in her greeting as she met me at the door. Her wisened eyes gave me the "Carbon 12" test as she pressed for a decision. "Are you Catholic or a Pentecostal?"

It was as if I had to make a decision right there. Grandma Mason just couldn't believe that they might go together—Catholic and Pentecostal. The Lord anointed my tongue with a quick coining, "I guess I am a Cathacostal."

I got into the meeting on the password. It was my turn to be amazed at the power, the holiness, and the openness to my further sharing the good news—a Catholic can both be saved and filled with the Holy Spirit.

There was much to write home about that summer in Carolina. From my new highrise at A & T I typed up three whole sheets as a summer epistle one day and asked the girl in the office to run off forty copies of each.

By mistake she ran off eighty. "Oh, no!" I thought.

"Oh, yes!" God confirmed.

There was a momentary battle within. How could I share these incredible miracles with people who hadn't seen them and who would most likely reject the tale as a "whopper" and me as a "crazy." Again God seemed to say, "Trust Me."

Taking my address book I prayed over the names, and quickly settled for the eighty I believed God was asking me to share this letter with. It still seemed such a daring thing to do. The envelopes were stuffed with the "good news."

At a prayer breakfast that day I found myself asking for prayers that the "folly" feeling be lifted. God not only lifted the feeling but assured through a prophet, "You think that this was your idea. No, I tell you that it was My idea in the first place that you might share My mighty works. Nor was it a mistake that the copies were doubled for I have ordained everyone who will receive this letter and everyone who will read it. I will cause it to be anointed and multiplied yet more as it is read. For I will have My people know that I am doing a great thing and about to do a still greater thing across the face of the earth."

When I returned to Minnesota and Iowa I picked up stories of how this letter had been read, passed on, and sent across the country. In my years away from home I had written many letters, but never before had I heard of one being passed around the neighborhood and sent across the country.

One night before I left Carolina the Lord used Doug Raye to minister in a word of knowledge about the particular gifts that the Lord had given to each of us. This was a new ball game for me and I wasn't sure how God was playing it or if He really was.

The results of my "testing the spirits" put me at the end of the prayer line with the conviction that God had a word of knowledge for me through Doug. With the directness of a power switch thrown the word came: "I have given you a gift of healing—not just physical healing but healing in the churches. I have given you a power over evil spirits. In My name you will cast them out. I have given you a gift of evangelism to go forth to spread My word and to think not of what you will say for I will give you the words . . ."

"But, but, but . . . God." I argued. Then I prayed, "God, how am I going to tell Mother Georgianne? And what will she say?"

I am aware of your concerns, of your every move. I know every time you take a breath; I know every time you turn your head, move your toe. I am with you and I'm concerned. I watch over you. I will not let you get hurt because My love wants to protect you.

Let Me come into every part of your life. You are holding Me out of certain parts of your life. My daughter, I don't think you comprehend what you mean when you pray, "Thy kingdom come." I want My kingdom to come, and I need you. Hurry along quickly, prepare yourselves that I may use you.

Chapter Ten
Lord of Your Life

By the following May it became increasingly clear that God was leading me, after twenty-six years in the classroom, out to another apostolate.

In January of 1971, at the Leader's Conference in Ann Arbor, Michigan, my "inner voice" began to be confirmed by some "outer voices." "Sister, you are not using the gifts the Lord has given you."

Three different times during that weekend conference these same words were spoken to me by three brothers from different parts of the country. None of them had ever met me before.

When the third spoke I knew that God was trying to tell me something. About a month later, pondering my discernment papers for the next year's teaching assignment, I found myself writing: I would like to be free to follow the work of the Holy Spirit. That was as simple and direct as I could state what I was hearing.

I don't know what I anticipated as a response, but I hardly expected what I got: "Write a job description."

"Hmmmm!" I said. "God, would You like to dictate a job description?" He lead me to two books: *The Bible* and *You Are Sent* (a just-off-the-press 1970 edition of the Acts of the Thirteenth General Chapter for the School Sisters of Notre Dame).

Approval was not immediate. Neither was disapproval. What was concretely open made me cringe and my Superior gasp: "Traveling with an inter-faith team across the United States in a 'revival USA' program."

No matter what the outcome, I knew that I needed to pursue the possibility. I was not at all certain that this was what God was calling me to, but I was powerfully sure that He was asking me to ask my Provincial Superior.

"If you really feel this is what God is calling you to, perhaps you had better consider following it outside of religious life. Have you ever thought that God might be calling you to leave religious life?" was the hard answer I received.

"No, I hadn't." To even think that it might be suggested hurt me deeply.

Back at the convent I was so crushed that before I could share what had happened with Sister Ethel, the other Spirit-filled nun in our convent, I suggested, "Let's pray first."

As we prayed the Lord anointed Sister with a word of prophecy: "Do not be shook. In a few days, I will give you more light . . . do not weep . . ."

In a few days there was more light and more challenge. I did not weep. "I think that you should talk to the Bishop about this," was the next suggestion.

Bishop Waters' response first by mail and then by conference was prompt, positive, and encouraging. He wrote, "I think that all of us ought to re-examine what we are doing in light of what the Holy Spirit is asking us to do today. I'll see you on Monday."

On Monday he shared: "I see no reason why you would experience difficulty sharing the work of Catholic Charismatic Renewal across the United States. The

Bishops in November of 1969 have come out with a statement affirming the work. In summary, they found the Pentecostal movement in the United States scripturally and theologically sound, and the fruit of the movement was judged good. Their conclusion was "that the movement should at this point not be inhibited but with prudence allowed to develop."

Much encouraged, I took the plunge out of high school teaching into full-time work in Charismatic Renewal. As I left Loyola I recall one of the priests sharing: "Sister, I really believe in all that you have shared with me and in all that you are doing. But for me it is like it is His kingdom against mine." Quickly he realized what he had said. And so did I.

With summer came an invitation from Father Jim Ferry to spend the summer with the H.O.P.E. (House Of Prayer Experience) community in Goshen, New York. What better place than a charismatic House of Prayer in order to grow and discern where the Lord would lead. There could be little doubt about His leading, for the day I was traveling the last lap from Minnesota to New York the Scripture reading of the Mass at St. Vincent's in the Bronx confirmed: "I will lead you into the land of Goshen."

Much happened at H.O.P.E.—much of the good, the true, the startling, and the unbelievable. I could not doubt the love of Jesus calling to a deeper repentance, deeper union, and seeking His will in a special work of charismatic renewal in His church. My response remained simple: "Yes, God, and praise God!" We followed through a program that was completely Jesus-orientated.

Many things happened that summer.

One day Shelley Cohen, Jewish pianist for the *Tonight Show,* shared the noon liturgy with us.

He also shared his testimony. Shelley had just come to Christ. Some of his Catholic neighbors had invited him to a Life in the Spirit seminar. He went. Shelley found himself asking questions he had never asked before. He found himself getting answers he had never gotten before. Going back to his Jewish elders he questioned, "What do you believe?"

He discovered they did not even believe in a personal God. To stay with the old was death. To accept the new was death of another sort. Finally he decided on the death that led to being born again.

After Communion that day, Shelley said, "Every time I come to worship the Lord I think I've got all that I can hold and then I discover that there is so much more." Shelley experienced some of that in a word of prophecy: "My son, I know that you have given up everything. But I will give it back to you, pressed down, heaped over, and flowing over the top."

Several days later Shelley and his wife, Leona, were back to discover still more. As we shared soup and sandwiches in our camp dining room, they expressed some concern because this was the day they had chosen to go back to their Jewish friends to share this new experience but somehow they were grieviously afflicted with headaches that nothing could lift or help.

"Do you know that Jesus could lift that?" I asked.

"You've got to be kidding."

"No, really it is very simple for Jesus to take away the pain."

After lunch the three of us sat out on the rugged bench of the camp kitchen and lifted our minds to the Lord, I rested my hand on Shelley's head, asked Jesus to take the pain, and the pain was lifted! "Incredible! Wow! What a God we serve!" Shelley rejoiced.

"To show you that I had nothing to do with it, Shelley,

you rest your hand on your wife's head and ask the Lord to take her pain." He did. And God did.

A new Shelley has been playing for an old show. From behind the scenes Shelley writes, "I am writing new songs that I had never dreamed I could write. I am writing words to songs—a thing that I could never do before my baptism in the Holy Spirit."

Though my experience was some nineteen months hot, cold, or old—to many people I was still in the "cage" stage. For the sake of newcomers Father Jim often chided me, "Fran, cool it. Keep the lid on."

It wasn't easy but I was learning. I learned that no matter how high the Lord has escalated you, you need to be sensitive to the feelings of those who haven't yet stepped on to the escalator, or maybe don't care to.

Many old truths took on a new relevancy that summer. There was much to relearn about "walking in the Spirit" that savored of teaching we had had way back in our Novitiate days. I was experiencing it with a new sense of high adventure and an experiential realization that we serve a "fun God."

One of the most fascinating days I spent in the House of Prayer was a "Hermit Day." The plan was to spend the whole day away from the rest of the community, alone before God, without even a Bible for a guide. Just the thought: "God is and I am!"

About eight in the morning I began the day sitting on the floor in our little chapel room. I had a lot of unwinding to do . . . or to let God do. Only at about ten o'clock could I say, "It's all right, God, that I do not have a thought in my head but that You are here and I am here."

As twelve hours ticked away, a deeper and deeper peace settled upon me, which told me that there had been a lot of noise in me in spite of the quiet of our House of Prayer. As the day finished I sat with a blank page over my closed

Bible thinking, "I've got to have something to share with the communtiy tomorrow . . . something that the Lord has taught me in this day of stillness."

At the end of an hour I was still sitting on the floor. And the page in front of me was still blank. A little indignant, I turned to God for an explanation. "Is this all that I can say this day has taught me? Twelve hours before you and all I can share is a blank page!"

Then God spoke. "Yes. The blank page is all the message. That is the way I want you to come before me every day—like a blank page. And when you stop writing on it what you want Me to do with your life then I will indeed be Lord of your life!"

I will open for you every door I want and close those I do not want . . .

When you are beset by doubts, know that I am still here. These plans are My plans, not yours. You've asked to be used by Me and I've told you that I will use you. The plan is Mine to work out. I've not given the plan to you.

I'm only asking you to be My tool. The hammer does not know what the carpenter is doing. It only follows the hand of the carpenter. I will pick you up and I will lay you down. When I need you I will use you. I know what I am doing. I know what I am building. All I ask is that you be on hand when I need you.

Because I have called you a hammer, do not think that I despise you. A carpenter loves his tools and the more he loves them, the better he handles them and the better work they will do for him.

I have many tools. They are arrayed before Me and I pick the one I need. Be content to lie still if I do not need you, for I know where you are. And I will pick you up when I need you.

Chapter Eleven
Open Doors
and Closed Doors

God is sometimes called "the Lord of the eleventh hour." With the last mail of my stay in Goshen came the printed word from my Superiors, "Permission is granted to work out a 1971 to 1972 assignment in consultation with the Provincial Team."

It was the first of a new kind of obedience which would allow for following a move of the Spirit which was not only different, but in many respects unpredictable.

With this permission I was free to follow through a lot of open doors to share with Catholic and Ecumenical prayer groups, in Protestant churches, at Full Gospel Businessmen's conferences, and to give a nun's witness at the International Assembly of God conference in Chicago.

For the latter, Sister Brigid, my coordinator of Apostolate, was a bit leery (as I myself was) about what I might be sharing with these ministers of the gospel, so she asked to see a copy of my talk. I was relying on that word of prophecy as it was spoken to me the summer before in North Carolina, " . . . think not what you will say for I will give you the words."

But Sister Brigid wanted to see those words. So I promised an outline, which I faithfully made of all the safe things a Catholic nun might say to Assembly of God

ministers and the things my Superior would readily understand and approve. But when the day came for the talk,
in no way could I relate to that outline. In no way could I
remember anything except another prophetic word that
had been given me in Goshen, "You have given Me your
heart; now give Me your mind."

With reckless abandon, I threw away the outline, gave
Him my mind, and stood before that International Assembly of ministers without an organized thought in my head.
"I feel like little David with a slingshot and a couple of
pebbles in the land of giants." That is all I remembered
saying when I quit an hour and a half later.

God did something that day. Two of the leading men of
the conference, Dr. Quanabusch and Dr. Rasmussen,
shared with me later that they had wept all through the
talk as they realized how God was pouring out His Spirit
on a Church they had studied only as "the whore of
Babylon."

It was this experience that opened the doors for overseas
evangelism in Sweden with the Full Gospel Businessmen,
and in South America, Israel, and around the world with
the World Thrust team. It opened doors but also closed
them, for it was the discernment of the Provincial Team
that it would be wiser for me to become more strongly
grounded in Catholic Pentecostalism before I got too involved in the ecumenical. It was suggested that I check out
living for a time in the Word of God community in Ann
Arbor, Michigan.

I knew that there was a really good thing going on in
Ann Arbor, but my human spirit cried out, "Not that,
Lord! Not for me!" This was by far the most Abrahamic
thing I had ever been asked to do and not to do. The call to
"evangelism" was very much alive; so was my rebellion.
Had I persevered in my rebellion, I would have missed one
of the biggest blessings of my life, living for nineteen months in the Word of God community.

At this time the whole Pentecostal phenomenon was quite foreign to our Provincial team, so Sister Brigid decided to spend several days with me as a guest of the Word of God community. Many things in the Gary Morgan household impressed Sister, but her overall impression of the community was, "I have never seen such holiness in young people." It was this that sealed the decision that I was free to decide to live in the Word of God community despite the fact that there was no promise of a job (in November in a university town) or of getting into a Christian household (there was a waiting list), but there was Jim Cavnar's word of faith, "Come and see!"

I found myself "the flying nun" en route to Michigan to "come and see." On this plane the Father reached down with a Word as recorded in Isaiah 41 some 3,000 years before, " 'Do not fear, for I am with you; do not look anxiously about you, for I am your God. I will strengthen you, surely I will help you. Surely I will uphold you with My righteous right hand . . . For I am the Lord your God, who upholds your right hand, who says to you, Do not fear. I will help you' " (verses 10 and 13).

To show further what a provident Father God is, about a year before I moved to Ann Arbor, He spoke to Art Griffith, a Full Gospel Businessman from Battle Creek, Michigan, about "adopting" me as a spiritual daughter. This was at that first convention in Chicago when I knew only a few of the hundreds of Businessmen I now know in the Fellowship. I always did love that promise: "And everyone who has left houses or brothers or sisters or father or mother or children or farms for My name's sake, shall receive many times as much, and shall inherit eternal life" (Matthew 19:29).

There is no telling how much grace and power has flowed to me and from me because a spiritual father and mother are moved to pray for me daily. Sometimes in his prayers Art used to say, "Lord, does Sister Fran need money?" Then he would ask, "How much?" Days later there would be some special need that I would see the money was meant for.

Living in the Word of God community, one quickly found that this was more than a name; it was a way of life. It was our way of praising God, of relating to our brothers and sisters, of solving problems, of providing both the plan and the power of growth. It was the way our community of 700 took on the appearance and the power of Christians living in the early Church. It was our way to a deeper and deeper discovery of the reality of Jesus and the power of the Holy Spirit changing our lives.

During my stay I lived in three different households, each for six months—an Ecumenical at 1327 Broadway, a household of girls in the Fuller Apartment, and with the Ted Kennedy family at 1608 Granger. Each was progressively powered and unique in a season of change and growth.

At least twice daily in our households we shared in some way the Word of God as we shared prayer in the early morning and the late evening. Besides this we were urged to have an hour of personal prayer when we allowed the Lord to teach us more directly through the Word. Often what He taught us in that time of quiet we shared in a once-a-week morning of Bible sharing.

During the evening meal we were encouraged to do faith-sharing of how we had experienced or missed God in our lives that day. This may sound formidable to newcomers, but once one caught the power and the ease of it, it made better sense to be sharing the Good News than the bad. One day someone "blew our minds" with the rhetorical question: "What in the world did we ever talk about before we talked about Jesus?"

I have never seen such a group of turned-on-for-Jesus

and tuned—out-of-this-world Christians as I have come to know in the Word of God community. I have never seen such holiness in both young and old. I have prayed for many . . . and with many. Always there has been a lot of give and a lot of take. It takes being there, experiencing this different life to appreciate what is going on in oneself, in others, and in the church. Contrary to a rumor that is sometimes circulated about the charismatic experience or about charismatic communities, it is not a highly emotional but rather a healthy, holy milieu where people freely express feelings about life, about themselves, and about God.

As with many things, misunderstanding and judgment come as a matter of semantics or superficial knowledge rather than reality. If emotional means being enthusiastic, I have seen it, I have been it, and it has been good! If emotional means being excited about God because He is great, unfathomable, present, I have seen it, been it, and prayed for it. If emotional means sharing God and the Word of God on a twenty-four hour basis, I have seen it, heard it, and spoken it. If emotional means brothers and sisters greeting with a genuine sign of affection—a Christian hug—I have seen it, experienced it, and grown with it. It is a proven way to break down the fears, the prejudices, and the barriers that separate us from each other and from God.

Living in the Word of God community, I was a long time growing in the vision, the dream, and the reality of what God is doing to build His House, to renew His Church, to prepare His bride. Members were active in some forty services: pastoral, administrative, teaching, and works of mercy. The biggest project was the one the Lord was sovereign in—the changing of people's lives.

To the women He spoke: "I am changing things within you that you thought would never change, and don't expect this to stop. And I tell you, long have I desired, long have I hungered and thirsted to do this with a group of women. Since the beginning of time I have hungered to do this with My women; this is the first time on the face of the earth that I have been able to do it. You are the women of My promise and of My covenant, and I will make you holy and perfect."

To the community at large He spoke: "I have only begun . . ." Over the whisper of some one thousand worshippers at a Thursday night prayer meeting God spoke in promise: "I will make of you a mighty shout to the nations and as yet you are but a whisper."

Be with Me. I only want that you yield more and more . . . to be with Me always. I have asked that you be with Me always, just as I am with you always. I want you to be My vessel of praise. I want you to live in My praise and to draw others to Me by praising Me.

I am asking you to yield. My prophecies are living words. As I speak, My Word is being accomplished. I am a living God. My Words are living. Remember always that I am your God and I'm looking after you.

Chapter Twelve
Talk About Tongues

On the outside looking in—I was against it. You might say that I was down on what I was really not up on. Even when I had reached that moment of enlightment, hunger, and emptiness to know that I wanted the baptism in the Holy Spirit, I also knew I wanted it without tongues.

At that time I had read somewhat, and came to fear somehow, that if I accepted this gift it might control me at the most undesirable times to my supreme embarrassment—like some day during the common prayer in our convent chapel. I actually feared that while others prayed in English, I would suddenly spill out a volley of words in other tongues. Now I wonder that I could have been so ignorant.

And still today this is one of the questions I am amazed to have people ask again and again: "Do you mean to tell me that you can just start and stop this language any time you want?"

It was only a month after my initial experience of being prayed with for the baptism in the Holy Spirit that I realized I was missing something by not having this gift of tongues.

In 1969 I attended the Catholic Charismatic Leaders

Conference. At the beginning someone announced that no one was in charge of directing the meeting, except the Holy Spirit. Everyone was encouraged to be sensitive to the Spirit leading as Paul described in I Corinthians 14:26: "When you assemble, each one has a psalm, has a teaching, has a revelation, has a tongue, has an interpretation. Let all things be done for edification." I remember how impressed I was as the meeting took off with spontaneous prayer, Scripture, prophecy, interpretation, a vision, all merging into one theme—God's love.

That night I saw and heard for the first time the power of an assembly praising God in tongues. I knew for the first time that I was missing something. From all around me rose sounds of praise in languages I had never heard, in a harmony that was out of this world.

"Lord, I change my mind about those tongues, I'll take them."

It was just a fleeting thought, a prayer—and nothing happened. Later that night I truly repented for having regulated for God how many gifts He was free to release in my life.

My repentance bore fruit. I awoke in my sleep that night saying strange words—first one, then another, and another! Suddenly I realized what I was doing—I was praying in tongues. I got so excited I demanded: "God, what did I say?" And He gave me the interpretation: "Oh, my loving Father."

This has always been most meaningful to me because it explains what the gift of tongues is—crying out to our loving Father in a thousand ways our human mind cannot conceive—telling Him how loving He is, how worthy of our thanksgiving, of our worship.

That day and for many days that followed I prayed over and over that phrase in tongues—knowing it was the Spirit of the living God crying out in worship of the Father. I remained in the primer stage of "Oh, Oh!" for perhaps a month or more.

Finally one day I realized I was tired and embarrassed of being only a few-words tongues speaker. I was becoming more and more frustrated. In disgust one day I cried out, "God, I am not saying another word until You do." I waited and waited and waited! Determined to have a word without breaking mine, I cut the Scripture. God's word hit me, not only right in the eye, but in the pit of my stomach: "Though it tarries, wait for it, for it will certainly come, it will not delay" (Habukkuk 2:3).

Several days later at one of our youth meetings, Jim McInnes, now leader of a Jesus House in Joteborg, Sweden, challenged me. "Sister, will you pray for a very special need of mine?"

"Sure, Jim," I promised, not thinking that it would be a lot easier to pray if I knew what he wanted prayer for. The next morning I woke up at about three with a sense of urgency — "I've got to pray for Jim but I don't know what the problem is." I complained, "Now, Lord, if I could pray in tongues, You who knows Jim's, problem might give me the words."

It was hardly more than a thought but with it came power. From my inner being words came pouring forth like a torrent. Sounds and syllables gushing like a river! Strange but not weird. Foreign and yet from the very core of my being. On and on I prayed. Suddenly I had a sense that Jim's need—and mine—had been met. My "primer" stage was over—I was freely and fully praying in other tongues.

Like a little child with a new toy, I spent that next day praising God in my new prayer language for everything I could think of.

That evening I heard from Jim that my prayer had been

answered—postponement from military service to work in the ministry.

I had discovered another basic need and use for praying in tongues: praying for other people's problems. "And in the same way the Spirit also helps our weakness; for we do not know how to pray as we should, but the Spirit Himself intercedes for us with groanings too deep for words; and He who searches the hearts knows what the mind of the Spirit is, because He intercedes for the saints according to the will of God" (Romans 8:26-27).

Sometime ago I was referred to one of our retired Sisters who had suffered for a period of about three months with a feeling of tenseness, a horrifying pressure on the chest and neck, and a feeling that she couldn't breathe. The feeling never left by day or by night. Occasionally Sister would get a bit of relief from medication but the tormenting feeling always came back with the fear that she was not only losing her power to breathe but also her power to think. Often at night she would get up and go to the window, desperately hoping to get air. Often there was the sensation of someone attempting to choke her.

Sister asked for prayer. Not knowing how to pray, I prayed in tongues with the feeling that I was taking authority of the oppressing spirit in the name of Jesus. During the prayer Sister suddenly felt freed. The weight lifted and the oppression was gone.

When I meet Sister now, she glows. "That thing has never come back."

And I glow. "And it never will."

There is something about tongues in our combat with Satan. It is possible that we not only put him to flight but we leave him in confusion when we use tongues as a weapon. He knows it is like an A-bomb against him. This could be a reason why the enemy is ever ready and persistent to convince us that our prayer language is not real. He cannot rob us of the gift but he can work every mischief to keep us from using it or to render it ridiculous.

The summer I spent in Goshen was a summer of languages of praise. I used to sit out on a bale of straw on the slopes of the Catskills praising God by the hour in many tongues. Sometimes I would ask to praise in languages few people praise in and I would find myself praising in the strangest tongues. I came to sense a real difference between the music of the Oriental, the heaviness of the Slavic, and the abounding vowels in the Hebrew.

Paul says "If I speak with the tongues of men or of angels . . ." It is my belief that the more we freely yield and allow ourselves to exercise this gift we too can speak both with the tongues of men and of angels. Both in English and in tongues we only learn to pray by praying.

If there is one pattern in the mystery of tongues, I think it is that the Spirit often yields the language to fit the need of some particular person for whom we might be praying. One day as I was praying for a beauty operator, Gen suddenly looked up and exclaimed: "Sister, that word you just used, 'Macushla'. That is Gaelic for 'my loved one, my cherished one.' My mother used to call me that all the time."

Once in our House of Prayer at Convent Station, Robbie, a Spirit-filled Jewess, asked for prayers as she was about to make an important call to her parents. Robbie was concerned about saying loving things to parents who just couldn't understand why she would forsake the family heritage for this thing about Jesus and the Holy Spirit. As we prayed, my English quickly blended into another tongue. Robbie later identified that tongue as Hebrew; she understood for she studied it both here and in Israel. The words of petition she said were words that only a young Jewess would say to Yahweh and they were followed by Yahweh's consoling words to Robbie with a precision of meaning that only the Hebrew tongue could express to a young Jewish girl.

In May of 1973 I was asked to give a teaching on healing after one of the May devotions in the Catholic Church in Flint, Michigan. Sister Lucienne was with me to share a time of praying with people for healing after the talk.

In that crowd was a mother and father who had brought their baby for healing. The baby had a network of tubes in his mouth and nose. Moved with compassion I prayed knowing how Jesus loved little children. Later that evening the parents shared that before I prayed with their baby I had been praying in another language, but when I began praying with their baby I prayed in Polish. And they were Polish.

Tom was one of my friends from the Federal Correctional Institution in Milan, Michigan. Even after we had prayed with him for the baptism of the Holy Spirit with the evidence of speaking in tongues, Tom had unusual difficulty believing that his gift could be real. Besides having been caught up in the world of psychology, philosophy, and linguistics, Tom had had a rather unusual pastime of mimicry games with languages. In spite of his doubts Tom found himself one day sharing with conviction his experience of the baptism and tongues with an Indian prisoner who shared his dorm. The Indian found the whole thing quite illusory.

That night as they were lying on their bunks, Tom, not realizing what he was doing, let himself go on a line of tongues. The next thing Tom knew, the Indian repeated the whole thing and added a bit more. "What do you think you are doing?" Tom demanded.

"Well, you just have been praying in my Indian dialect —'Praise, most excellent praise to the Most High God;' and so I repeated it and added the forever and ever. Amen."

To me, praying in the Spirit or in tongues is the most intelligent thing I can possibly do for I am simply surrendering my human thought to the divine thought . . . my finite intelligence to infinite intelligence.

For many people, this is a mind-blower. But in the best sense of the word, we do well to allow our minds to be blown by the breath of God. Many unthinking people today are allowing their minds to be blown by the powers of evil in mind expansion, ESP, SIMS, horoscopes, and other occult practices to their own destruction.

If yielding to tongues seems like a foolish thing to do, perhaps our choice is that of being wisely foolish or foolishly foolish. It is no "foolish game God's Spirit plays with us," save the foolishness of the first Pentecost, the foolishness of Pope John praying for a new Pentecost: "Renew Your wonders in this our day as by a new Pentecost."

For those who have somewhat of a problem in releasing the gift, of "letting go and letting God," I would like to share a few simple things the Lord has taught me as I have assisted and encouraged many in releasing the gift.

From the start it is good to keep in mind what the Lord had to say about the gift. In Mark 16, we read that the Lord had just reproached the Eleven for their incredulity and obstinacy in believing those who had seen Him after He had risen. "And He said to them, 'Go into all the world and preach the gospel to all creation . . . These signs will accompany those who have believed: in My name they will cast out demons; they will speak with new tongues'."

It is always good to note He did not say these signs will follow *some* who believe, but *those* who believe. Nor did He promise that *some* will speak in other tongues, but "*they* will speak." They will if they will to. The Lord's word suggests that anyone who chooses to believe and anyone who chooses to speak will have this marvelous gift of praise.

Note that it is always referred to as a gift. Therefore it is not something one earns or deserves because of a certain state of holiness, but something one is free to expect, for it has been promised. And something one can readily ask for and then simply accept in faith.

We say to the Lord, "Give me."

And He says, "Take it."

Take for most people does not mean some kind of miraculous happening we often hear witnessed about. It simply means taking the Scriptural word for truth: "If you then, being evil, know how to give good gifts to your children, how much more shall your heavenly Father give the Holy Spirit to those who ask Him?" (Luke 11:13)—and the manifestation or evidence of speaking in tongues.

Take means believing the Word from Psalm 81:10: "I, the Lord, am your God . . . open your mouth wide and I will fill it." And so as we take that deep breath to breathe in the power of God and breathe out His word, we can expect things to happen. It might help to remember that praying in tongues is 100 percent God and 100 percent you. It is God's thought. It is your human anatomy. You don't have to have a thought in your head, for your prayer is His thought.

If you maintain a stiff jaw and a stiff upper lip when you pray or speak in English you are going to have an unlovely, distorted, impaired speech coming forth from your mouth. You will discover this is also true as you pray in tongues.

The more free and relaxed in God you can let yourself be, the more easily the Holy Spirit can use your being as a vessel of pure praise.

Take means "taking off," as when you were a little child and didn't know how to pray like the rest of the family, so you let yourself go with a lingo of babble. "Unless we become like little children . . ."

I remember encouraging one of the college girls, who was having difficulty releasing the gift, to just kneel by the bed and be again that little child taking off with a child's babble because she didn't know what to say to her loving Father. After about a minute, she was so anointed with the release of that heavenly tongue that all she could say between the flow of words was, "I can't stop. I can't stop. It's real. It's really real. Praise you, Jesus."

When I was in Sweden, the Lord taught me a simple truth about tongues. Whenever people of any language background say the word *Hallelujah*, that is already tongues, for it is the same in every language.

So whether you are a person who has never prayed in tongues, a person with a few words, or a person with just one prayer language and you would like to pray in many languages, just allow yourself to say a few times in a spirit of worship and praise that word *Hallelujah*! Hallelujah! Use it as a launching pad, allowing yourself to follow through with any new pattern of sounds and syllables such as you have never let go of before. But no English. You cannot pray in two languages at the same time. Stop one to start the other. Be so free that you are not even aware of the sounds that are coming forth from your lips after *Hallelujah*.

Take means keeping your eyes upon the Giver, not the gift. Think of yourself as a guitarist and picture what happens as you begin strumming until all at once you realize these sounds, these chords, are more than just sounds and chords—a melody is coming forth. A real melody is being born with words. It's happening—out of you is coming a song—your song.

It's like that with tongues. First just those sounds, those chords, that Presence, and then all of a sudden it is more—much more. You have released a gift. You've got it. The gift of tongues is yours. You are praising God in power with the mind of the Spirit!

No matter what your hang-up is, "Give your hang-up to Him who hung up for all of us," as Wendell Wallace has phrased it. And you will find that He who spoke the whole of creation into being can surely loose your tongue to speak the language of the Spirit.

Jesus cried out, "If any man is thirsty, let him come to me and drink. He who believes in me . . . From his innermost being shall flow rivers of living water. But this He spoke of the Spirit, whom those who believe in Him were to receive; for the Spirit was not yet given because Jesus was not yet glorified" (John 7:38,39).

The living water flowing from the very depths of your spiritual being is that free flow of syllables, sounds and words. The sounds are more than just sounds. The syllables are more than just syllables—coming from deep within you. Each syllable is like one of Peter's steps on the waters—suddenly you realize it's real. It is the Lord bidding you to speak . . . to walk. He is giving you the sounds, not from your mind but from the depths of your being. He is speaking His thoughts as the Spirit wells up within you and overflows in volleys of praise.

In Isaiah 55, we read: "Ho! Everyone who thirsts, come to the waters; and you who have no money, come . . . Let the wicked forsake his way, and the unrighteous man his thoughts; and let him return to the Lord, and He will have compassion on him; and to our God, for He will abundantly pardon. For My thoughts are not your thoughts.

neither are your ways My ways," declares the Lord (verses 1,7,8).

I would never contend that speaking in tongues is better or deserves more attention than any of the other gifts. Nor does it hold any promise of making you better than anyone else—just better than you are. This is one gift designed for our personal use, sanctification, and edification, and I for one can use all the edification I can get.

Often I found it good to allow the Lord to give me themes for praising Him in tongues. In this way, I can quickly learn to pray not just in the Spirit, but to pray with some understanding.

"I shall pray with the spirit and I shall pray with the mind also; I shall sing with the spirit and I shall sing with the mind also" (1 Corinthians 14:15).

Using themes can serve as a creative way of prayer and as a faith-builder for those who have difficulty in believing their tongue is real. If you were to praise God for your salvation, you would perhaps find the flow of words very different from the flow that might come if you were to praise Him for your baptism in the Holy Spirit.

Themes for praising God are almost as infinite as God: His goodness, His mercy, His boundless love, His endless forgiveness, His incomprehensible desire to share His life with us, His coming again. More and more I wonder how we ever got along without this new dimensional gift of praise.

On getting up in the morning I find slipping off a bit of tongues is a powered way of breaking down any resistance to the beginning of a new day in a spirit of worship (rather than a series of "Oh, nos" and the all-American grunts and groans!). Praying in tongues doesn't depend on how I feel, or whether my mind is up to it. With a theme such as thanking Him for what the night has been and for what the day will be—we've got it made.

Strange as it may seem, sometimes a song in the Spirit—in tongues—is the thing that can most easily set the tone for a Praise the Lord day! Psalm 96 says, "Sing to the Lord a new song; Sing to the Lord, all the earth. Sing to the Lord, bless His name . . . For great is the Lord, and greatly to be praised" (verses 1,2,4).

Cardinal Suenens once referred to the gift of tongues as "one of those lovely surprises of the Holy Spirit that no one was looking for, but now that it is here, let us enjoy it."

For this gift, as for all the gifts, I believe no one has all the answers, insights, or the last word, for we are all very much in the process of discovering, learning, and coming into the revelation of the Revelation. What is mystery we should be content to accept as mystery. Let our joy be in the gradual lifting of the veil, the peeping at the Infinite, the hearing of what is out of this world.

Poor God! First He had the dull fisherman. And now He has us. We set up such barriers to a way He would up-date our twentieth-century prayer experience. It seems that the older we get, the more barriers we set up and the more hang-ups we have. The younger we are, the closer to the "push-button" generation, the more we can follow this simple logic: If there are push-buttons for light, darkness, heat, cold, going up, coming down, recording, erasing, calling near, calling far, starting jobs, finishing them, entertaining, being entertained, if there is instant food and instant drink, then it just makes sense that there should be an instant language for praising the Lord!

I am the healer. I will heal in little ways and in big ways. My power is a balm. Use it lavishly. It will soothe. There will be no scar or disfigurement left. My healing will be complete.

Do not presume to judge My work. You see only the surface. How can you possibly know what I am doing? Do not question affliction; it is the afflicted who turn to Me. Do not question the timing; the timing is Mine.

There is so much I want to accomplish. Don't fear. I will use you. Continue to place yourselves in My hands . . . in My care. You may mistrust yourselves but never mistrust Me. I am faithful; the gift is Mine. I have given it to you. Be at ease, be comforted. Be sure of My love, My power, My care for you. I am ever faithful.

Chapter Thirteen
Gilead's Balm

"God, You poured it in. Now pour it out."

That was all I said. I felt the surge of God's power pour forth from my hands to the gnarled, twisted, arthritic hands of the old Sister I was praying with, and those buckled joints unbuckled, the fingers straightened, and the hands became as soft as a baby's.

I didn't know a lot about healing, how to pray, how to believe, for I had never prayed with anyone before, expecting to see God's power work.

Father Bob and I had been sharing about our work among the blacks. We shared a burden, a vision, and a desire to see what we were beginning to experience come alive among them. To hear Bob tell of God's healing power as he had an altar call after his Sunday Mass was a *Wow!*

I knew from my work in Georgia and in North Carolina that there was a tremendous need, hunger, and openness among these people for the things of God, the power of God, and the experience of God! Doctrine was not the answer. The social gospel had been tried and found wanting. As we were sharing, Bob suddenly suggested, "Sister, I think the Lord would like me to pray with you for a special anointing for a ministry of healing."

A bit startled, even frightened, yet enthused, I found myself responding, "Whatever and whenever you think!" We checked timing. It seemed there was no time but the present moment. No sooner did Bob rest his hand on my head with a prayer of anointing when God's power shot through me as if I were a lightning rod. I couldn't deny that there was something there that had not been present before!

And still I was much the Thomas. The "buts" began. "But what if it doesn't work?"

"Don't be silly. You don't heal, the Lord does," Bob said.

"Hmmmm! It's that simple. But how will I know when to pray with people?"

Bob replied, "Whenever you see anyone suffering. If the Lord moves you or they ask, just reach out in love as Jesus did."

Again it seemed so simple. Just a matter of God's power reaching out to God's people to do God's work. And all I need do was reach a bit, pray a bit, believe a bit, and praise a lot!

My first work-out came at about midnight of the same day. A Sister from Texas and I made our way across the sidewalk from the convention hall to St. Mary's Convent. We intended to slip in unnoticed, but down the stairs hobbled a little old crippled Sister to greet us. I took one look at her hands and panicked. "Oh Lord! You wouldn't be expecting me to pray for her!"

It was just a thought. I tried to drown it out. Sister had been packing to leave the next day for her summer vacation.

We chatted about this, about the place, about the conference. Finally I got the courage to change the topic, or rather to get to the topic; "Sister, you really have arthritis, haven't you?"

Looking down at her gnarled old hands she said with a heavy brogue, "Suren' I guess you could say that I have it. And the doctors can't be doin' a thing about it exceptin' givin' me more pills!"

"Would you believe Jesus could heal you?" I volunteered almost apologetically.

"Indeed He could be doin' it, if He wanted to."

"Would you believe He would do it right now if we prayed for you?" Again I was marveling as much at the words that were coming out of my mouth as out of hers.

"Why, yes, He could. Do pray for me!"

We sat down in their little parlor and began to pray. As I put my hands on hers all I was moved to say was, "Lord, You poured it in. Now pour it out." Minutes later, or even seconds the gnarls were gone. The buckles were gone. The pain was gone. The arthritis was gone.

To paraphrase John 2:11, this was the first of the signs given by Jesus in the convent of St. Mary's at Notre Dame, Indiana, to let His glory be seen, and His Sisters believed in Him.

A week later I was moved to be partner to a second healing on the way to Chicago. Sitting next to an elderly lady on the bus, I made several futile attempts to engage in a bit of conversation. She finally turned to say, "I've had an operation on my left ear and I can't hear."

I asked, "Do you believe that Jesus could heal you?" Catching what I had said through a combination of lip reading and the good ear she replied, "Yes, He could."

"Right now?"

"Yes. Right now."

We prayed, and as our bus rolled down the mountain slopes of West Virginia, I reached over to put my hand on her ear. It was as if a gentle bolt of "healing vibes" shot through the deafened ear. Between the two of us, the rest of that trip was one jolly Greyhound prayer meeting.

Despite these first two manifestations of Jesus' healing power, in the next year there were many times when I turned "chicken," allowed human respect to dictate, or simply lacked that mustard seed of faith to believe that Jesus would heal. And so He didn't.

There were many faith-building times when I saw healing after healing. There were times when I prayed and nothing happened. More and more I came to know that my part was not to be concerned, to keep records or statistics, but simply to respond with compassion to people's needs, to pray the prayer of faith, and then to let go. I do recall that it was harder to believe for myself than for others. Perhaps this was because when I was the one hurting, suffering, or oppressed with the pain, there was an additional faith-hurdle to be jumped.

An experience I can hardly forget concerns a healing, my healing, while living in the House of Prayer Experience (H.O.P.E.) in Goshen. It was one of my days for sharing the cooking in a rather primitive camp kitchen on the premises of the Dominican Academy of Broadlea.

Sister Ann and I were in the throes of making toast on the gas-burning broiler when we discovered that for some reason it just wasn't lighting. After several attempts at lighting we smelled the gas, but nothing was happening. There was no flame. There was no heat. There would be no toast for the eighty Sisters we were scheduled to be serving in just a matter of minutes!

Thinking to take a quick look at what could be wrong, I was in the direct line of the broiler when suddenly, like a dragon spitting a ball of fire in my face, the gas exploded. My face, my head, my hair were engulfed in a ball of fire!

Immediately I recognized it as an oppression of Satan, and though the burning pain on my face and right hand was excruciating, I began praising the Lord. All the way to

112

the emergency hospital the only way to "keep my cool" and endure the pain was to pray in tongues. I remember apologizing to the driver for a need to pray out loud as we rushed along the mountainside.

I also apologized to the doctor who examined my eyes, gave the shots against infection, and treatment for the burns. Later he told me that as I lay agonizing on the examination table praying in tongues, his thought was, "This Sister must be from some foreign part."

About an hour later I was dismissed from the emergency with several pain prescriptions and allowed back to our prayer community to suffer it out. And suffer I did. One look in the mirror and I knew that with that holocaust look my whole summer could go up in smoke. Horrors! Our God is a consuming fire (I knew that!). But this!

In my panic I remembered that on one of the first days of our summer program we were given Luke 12:49: "I have come to cast fire upon the earth; and how I wish it were already kindled." What was God saying?

"They will lay their hands upon the sick and they will recover," I found myself saying to the group gathered in my bedroom to help. "I want you to pray for I believe that God will heal me." I caught the startled look, then the pity. Some had never prayed for any kind of healing much less the miracle I was looking for.

More out of pity than belief they began . . . suddenly I realized there was no more pain, no more burning. I was healed—I could throw away the pain prescriptions! It was incredibly true! I felt like Shadrach delivered from the fiery furnace . . .

My face still looked a mess. Two or three layers of skin peeled very gently in the next few days, but with dark glasses and a wig I was restored to the swing of the community the next day. Several days later, to everyone's amazement, including the doctor who had treated me, I had new skin for the new wine. And not a scar!

I often wonder about God setting up these little dramas so His people, like the eighty Sisters in the House of Prayer, could witness, perhaps for the first time, that He desires to heal *now*.

I also wonder what part the enemy played in the drama, for I remember the Sisters sharing with me that I missed out on an exciting bit of activity the night of my burning. While I spent that first day recuperating in bed, the others started putting together pieces of a puzzle. The night before my accident there had been an unexplained fire under the floor in that same kitchen where I had met my tragedy.

Suspecting old Sleuthfoot had a hand in both burnings, they burned him out that night with a celebrated liturgy in the adjoining room. Somewhere in the prayers Jim assumed authority over every spirit of evil that might be present in that place. There was a loud clanging of pans in the kitchen by unseen forces, then peace.

Besides quickening our faith this miracle quickened the desire to know more about healing. Several times before that summer the Lord had spoken to Sister Marilyn, a nurse from Hong Kong, Sister Rosemarie, from upper New York, and me about the gift of healing. So the three of us approached Father Jim. "Jim, we'd like some teaching on healing."

"Ask the Lord to give it to you."

Sitting on the floor of our prayer room, hands resting on the Bible we prayed, "Lord, You've spoken to each of us about this gift. Now we come asking; teach us to use it. We believe every word You said in this Book about healing. We praise You for every miracle of healing since the beginning of time. Whatever we don't know, we ask that You teach us. Whatever power we don't have, we ask that You give us." We prayed in the Spirit about ten minutes. Then listened as God began teaching in tongues with interpretation.

We gathered for about half an hour each day. What we continued to hear we tape recorded, first for us to study, now for you at the beginning of each chapter.

Only a few days passed before God sent us some "lab work"—a paralytic Sister of Charity with her left arm and the left side of her face paralyzed. The first day we saw no signs but we believed for God's timing, for God's way. The second day we saw no signs but we were thankful for what God was doing. The third day Sister encouraged, "People say I'm looking different." The fourth day we said, "Margaret, you are looking different." The fifth—the paralysis was completely gone.

"But when the multitudes saw this, they were filled with awe, and glorified God, who had given such authority to men" (Matthew 9:8).

My Blood is impenetrable. Only cover yourselves with it and you will be made whole. What power of evil will it not overcome? I am the Almighty God; My Blood has washed away all evil and conquered every evil power. I offer to you the cloak of My Blood. Wrap yourselves around with it; cover My people with it. If you only knew how powerful it is. It is a bulwark of power, safety, warmth, and love. Do not leave My children unprotected. The cloak of Blood is always ready for you. I hold it for you. Reach for it. Yield yourselves to Me. You do not realize the extent of My power and My love. You have put up barriers around your hearts but I will pull them down. And I will give you new hearts. I have told you that I am pleased with you but there is much left to be done. I am the Almighty.

Chapter Fourteen
Inner Healings

Sometimes we are given unusual insight into the reality and extent of the miracle of inner healing in others. This was the case with Tom, one of the men in the Federal Correctional Institution at Milan.

On our first trip to the prison we were introduced to Tom, a prisoner-assistant to the chaplain. On the surface he had a handsome billboard face, a "letterman" physique, and the makings of a politician, psychologist, and criminologist. As Tom shared, we came to know a man living without hope, despairing of all the traditional ways, means, and people programmed to help prisoners rehabilitate.

He could play the psychologists' games. NARA held a challenge some days, other days it killed and was killing. Transactional Analysis had lost its fun—"It was more comfortable before we knew where we were coming from." Religion was nothing more than a bunch of beliefs you either held to or you didn't. It didn't keep him out of prison and it wasn't helping him out now that he was in. Suicide was the most promising of the unpromising possibilities.

In this state of despair, Tom presented himself one day

to Father Granger. Father suggested, "Tom, did you ever think of asking the Sisters to pray with you for inner healing?" No, he hadn't, but he might.

He did. As we might do for anyone, we began with a bit of teaching and assuring, and then we prayed for inner healing. In the teaching it seemed good to summarize that man can be hurting in four ways: The sin area (God can forgive); demonic oppression or depression (God can free); the physical (doctors, medicine, and God can heal); the psyche or emotional (if we say that God cannot heal, we deny His power and if we say that God will not, we deny His love).

So the first fact stands: God *can* and God *wills* to heal us in the depths of our psyche.

Secondly, with God there is no such thing as time—the ten, twenty, or even fifty years ago. There is just the present moment. God can heal all the traumatic moments of the past in the present moment—our inner man hurt by sin, our own or others. He can heal the binding effects of our having been unloved, abandoned, rejected, betrayed, abused, punished. He can heal as He reveals the roots of our fears, our rebellions, our addictions. He can power us to seek forgiveness, and to forgive everyone who has hurt us.

As Tom listened he had none of the usual objections he often raised just to keep the conversation stimulating. Instead we sensed an eagerness to get with it.

So we did. For about an hour we prayed and as we did we walked back with Tom over the troubled waters of his life. Sister Lucienne and I took turns with whatever the Lord might give. Starting at the time of Tom's conception, claiming freedom from any bondage of another generation, we went on to claim God's love in the now for the past moments when Tom felt rejected, unloved, lonely, confused, anxious, fearful, rebellious. We prayed through basic

118

periods of time like the time before birth, the first five years, the grade school, the high school, the time after. Many thoughts fell in concerning relationships, feelings, attitudes, patterns of thought, addictions. In all of this we did not really know Tom, except as one of the prisoners who had come for help.

But God knew Tom. God led us to pray the right words, to bring forth the right ideas, to uncover the realms of darkness. After prayer we knew that whatever God wanted to do for Tom He had done!

Only several weeks later when we took Tom out on a church trip did we discover the extent of what God did that day. "As you were praying," Tom related, "I saw as it were on a TV screen, picture after picture from my past life that I had never admitted to my conscious mind because it hurt too much, and with it went the feeling that I had never allowed myself to feel, because it hurt too much. I saw it; I felt it. And then it was burned up! And there was another! This went on, not only for the whole hour that you were praying for me, but for several weeks after. I would have a flash of something else God was healing. Then one day I realized I was a different Tom. I was completely healed in my inner being. I knew the peace of Jesus!"

God began using Tom with some of the most hopeless cases in the prison, men with whom no one could communicate. Tom said, "I would find myself saying 'God, what's it with this man?' God would show me and we would have a thing going." People couldn't get over it. They wanted the secret.

The secret is penetrating more and more circles, touching mysteries and bondages not just from our times, but from other generations. As I prayed for the inner healing of Gene Lilly, a man from Orlando, Florida, recently healed from seventeen years of multiple sclerosis, I happened to say, "And I take authority on any witchcraft from another generation . . ." At that moment Gene had been given a vision of Indians in witchcraft dance. He remembered then his Indian ancestry. Only then did we wonder if there was some connection between a lifetime of MS and this bondage of witchcraft.

Perhaps the most bizarre but beautiful experience I've had in combining a ministry of inner healing with deliverance from witchcraft concerned a Spirit-filled girl we'll call Jean.

Before I met Jean at the weekend of Renewal where I was a speaker, Jean had been with, fallen from, and attempted to come back to the fellowship of a prayer group. As she shared with me her story of drugs, fears, and obsession with the occult, she also shared a particular experience that led her into incredible bondage.

This is Jean's story as related two years later: "About a year before I met you during a time when my mind was really obsessed with the occult, I found myself wandering about the streets of our city one night in a state of depression and rebellion. In that state I aimlessly wandered into a basement where a Black Mass was going on. To my dismay I was spotted as a good victim, drugged, and offered up in Satanic ritual.

"When I woke up at about three the next morning I was alone in this gruesome black room with its red candles extinguished, but still smelling of smoke, pot, and incense. Horror gripped me. Fear and despair deepened as I fumbled up the dingy basement steps staggering under a growing realization that I was no longer my own. Groping in my own madness and insane confusion I wandered about the streets and riverfront all day, several times attempting suicide.

"As night fell an even greater darkness descended, controlled, and drove me until I found myself in the chant, the scent, and the blackness of that basement of the night before. The Satanic High Priest was pleased. 'We will complete the offering.' Finally he announced, 'Finished. Now you belong wholly to Satan.'

"A horrifying exhilarating power began to control my mind and feelings giving me a dizzying sense of control over others. I thought power, I spoke power, I read power! Power controlled me! I used power to destroy others! Yet power was destroying me! I began to sense the living hell I was living in. Yet I had no power to be freed from it.

"Then one day someone in our prayer community discovered what had happened to me. With inexhaustible patience and love they began what came to almost a year of praying for me and with me but due to my stubbornness, fears, and obsessions, it was to no avail.

"Finally, Sister, the day I shared with you in the reception area I felt a deep and frightening feeling to run, to run fast and far. I felt the love of Jesus in you but I did not understand it nor did I know how to accept it until later that evening when you prayed with me for inner healing. I was definitely healed of past memories, of people who had hurt me, of my fears, and of an obsession with the occult.

"Today I am two years older. My spiritual growth is blossoming slowly and I know God loves me. My family situation which was very bad has become one of love, joy, unity and peace since I finally turned to God. Praise God!"

Sister Lucienne and I were led late one night or rather early one morning to share the ministry of inner healing with a special group of women gathered in the large motel room of the Winning Women's Retreat in Kalamazoo, Michigan. We just happened to mention how sometimes our need for healing goes back to being unwanted in our mother's womb. Immediately three women seated on the davenport identified: "I was that child."

As we prayed about other things the Lord led us to pray for the healing of their own unwanted pregnancies, the healing of their husbands, and of their children. Never have I sensed the power of God so present as I did that morning between one o'clock and three! After we finished the prayer, some of the women shared, "We have paid our psychologists and psychiatrists hundreds of dollars yet they haven't done what the Lord has done here this night! Praise God!"

Together with our need for inner healing, more and more we are beginning to realize our need to reach out with a word of forgiveness as we walk the streets, as we read our newspapers, as we realize the sins of our nation. We need to deliberately say, "I forgive you, I forgive you, I forgive you." And we need in specific situations to ask, "Will you forgive me?"

In one of our Charismatic retreats in Adrian, Michigan, this thought came very strongly to Sister Joan Conrad, one of our SSND missionaries to Japan. Sister Joan asked that we pray with her for an anointing so that she might go back to Japan in the name of our nation, and ask forgiveness for our having dropped the bomb. As we prayed the Lord confirmed this desire with a prophecy: "I am indeed calling you to a healing of the nations . . ."

In visiting the prison that Saturday we took Sister Joan along and asked that she share something of this with the men. As she shared we felt the tug of God asking us to seek forgiveness of the prisoners for the ways society had hurt them. They in turn were moved to ask our forgiveness for the ways they had hurt society. What a reconciliation! Only God could bring it to pass!

For some of the prisoners this healing has become particularized as in the case of convict John McClish. John wrote to Kilgrove, the banker from Leon, Iowa, after his conversion to ask for and receive forgiveness in the name of Jesus. John, only twenty-two, has served four years of his twenty-five year sentence for bank robbery. The first year and a half, according to one of the men, John was still a pretty tough customer for anyone who said the wrong thing or rubbed him the wrong way.

Then John had a Christmas Eve experience of accepting Jesus Christ. Not long after that John began studying for the ministry in the prison.

Today according to a recent article in the *Detroit News,* John the convict is being allowed to go out evenings escorted by a prison guard to preach the gospel at Calvary Baptist Church in Dundee. He says, "There is more to Christianity than being saved. Jesus wants to use us. When you wake up in the morning your first thought should be, 'What can I do for God today?'"

Such preaching presupposes much healing has taken place between John, God, and society. In John's last letter he wrote, "Things are going good here. Many souls are being saved, and all the glory belongs to Jesus alone!"

My kingdom is within you. My power is within you. My love is within you. Believe that I want to live in you. I want to show forth the glory of the Father in you.

I made man out of love. I became man out of love. I delight to be with man. My pleasure is that they be whole.

Think of what I have destined man for. Should he not be free in My love with nothing to bind him but My love? If you but knew what men are capable of in My love — perfection. I do not want men crippled and unfinished. This is not my work.

Who has done this to My people? Who has crippled them? Who has filled them with fear? Should you fear a God of love? Should you be in bondage? I will not stand for it. I will free them, for I am the Lord.

Chapter Fifteen
The Iceberg Melts

Psychologists tell us that ninety percent of what we are is buried in our subconscious, leaving only a tip of the psychological iceberg visible to ourselves and to others.

For many years the tip I allowed to be visible consisted of only the things a Sister wearing the holy habit and keeping the holy rule should think, say, or do. All the rest got buried in the great unknown.

In the summer of 1963 when I began my studies for an M.A. in Guidance and Counseling, I recall sharing one day with my instructor, "That class today was quite a revelation. I suddenly realized that I had enough raw material in my life for several breaks."

I cried a bit as for the first time I shared some of the deep feelings and thoughts I had never allowed to surface to my conscious mind about the tragic deaths the lonely years after, the fears of the future.

Seven years later some of these same feelings, thoughts, and fears surfaced again—this time with hope for an undreamed-of healing as I listened to Father MacNutt present a teaching on healing of memories.

After the lecture the line was long with people who desired prayer for inner healing. Finally, it was my turn to take my place on the wooden folding chair in the back room of St. Mary's basement.

"Father, I need inner healing from an incredible series of deaths that have hit my life. My mother died when I was thirteen. My father and my brother Gene when I was twenty-three. At thirty-three I almost died myself. And this past year my sister Laurie died in May, and my brother Ray in November."

As I continued to share I came to realize some of the depths of unspent grief, loneliness, and bitterness that had me torn and bound for twenty and thirty years. As Father prayed I came to realize that God was using him to speak even some of my unspoken thoughts and fears. All the while I was experiencing what I came to know as a conscious release from memories that sometimes plagued my waking and haunted my sleeping.

I don't know how it works; I only know it works. I had peace, joy, power, love, a feeling of wholeness as I had never known.

Over the past five years God has effected in me not just a work of inner healing but a work of deliverance that might be called cyclic, meaning it has come in successive waves of revealing, healing, freeing. Perhaps one reason why this healing and deliverance in most people is cyclic is that we could hardly handle the ninety percent in one transforming power-shot.

My first experience with deliverance was in the summer of 1970 in the main ballroom of the Chicago Hilton. After teaching Derek Prince announced: "Those who would like prayer for deliverance move over to this side of the room. Only those who have a need and a desire to be delivered move over there. You could get hurt by just staying on out of curiosity or unbelief."

My great desire to be an observer was thwarted. "If only I had something I could think of to be delivered from . . ." I searched myself in a panic.

Then from somewhere flashed the thought: "I'm not going to sit over there with the 'common herd'."

Immediately from somewhere else I was convicted of self-righteousness.

Quietly I moved over "there" with a feeling that was half-bold, half-timid, all the while hoping no one would notice one little nun in a blue suit with a black veil among the "common herd."

"Demons are addressed by their names," Derek shared. "Their names correspond to the compulsive behavior they attempt to inspire." With a deep assurance, I was freed that day from a spirit of self-righteousness.

My first deliverance was followed by a second completely unplanned, in the same conference room during the same week. Wendell Wallace had given the evening talk followed by a similar announcement: "Anyone desiring prayer come forward . . . for accepting Jesus, the baptism in the Holy Spirit, healing . . ."

"Why not!" I suddenly remembered a life-time battle with an anemic condition.

Nearing the front I was confronted by Demos Shakarian. "What would you like, Sister?"

"Prayer for an anemic condition." Demos had hardly touched my forehead when I fell backward under the power—slain in the Spirit for the second time that day. (The first was at the Kathryn Kuhlman session.)

Before I could register what had happened I heard within myself as clear as any voice I have ever heard, "I don't believe it. That wasn't any more real than when Kathryn touched me. It is all phony."

In the next second Wendell's voice boomed, "There is an unbeliever in the crowd. There is someone in this audience who does not believe. Will you please come forward to the microphone. Will the person who does not believe . . ."

I couldn't believe what I was hearing or what I was doing, for I was moving toward that microphone.

A black hand rested on my veiled head and Wendell prayed that I might believe. "Do you believe now, Sister?" he asked.

"Only with a belief because you prayed for me. But I don't feel any different."

"That you may believe there are two people in this audience with thoughts of suicide on their minds. Will they come forward?" They did . . . a man and a woman.

"Will all of you lift your hands for a minute and pray for this Sister?" A sea of hands raised toward me and like the sound of many waters a prayer rose.

"Is there a Catholic priest in the audience to pray with our Sister?" Father Bill came forward. I did not understand what was happening so I shared with him my want of understanding. After a soda we joined a small group for prayer in the upper lobby.

Father Bill began, "Jesus, You are the Lord. Uproot from Sister's heart this spirit of unbelief. Replace it with a spirit of faith."

I felt something going and I felt something coming. The sensation was that of a very gentle hand reaching in and pulling out a patch of deeply rooted weeds. Waves of power began to roll over me, causing my body to vibrate from head to foot. For the first time in my life I knew what it was to tremble under the anointing of God. For the third time that day I fell backwards under the anointing of the Holy Spirit. Three hours later I came to, murmuring, "Yes, God. Yes, God. Yes." I was surprised to hear myself saying, "Oh, He created a whole new heart in me and without a scar."

The next day someone shared: "As I raised my hand to pray for you, Sister, I realized it was the first time I had ever prayed for a Roman Catholic. As I did I sensed a real love and a healing between your church and mine." Many people shared a similar thought.

I remembered the prophetic word given me a few weeks before in North Carolina—"I have given you a gift of healing, not just physical healing but healing in the churches."

My growing into freedom has been a long journey . . . I am still traveling. I had my third experience of deliverance midway in the Foundation Courses at the beginning of my stay at Ann Arbor following a teaching on spiritual warfare. A small group of us met in the living room of the Cavnar home where leaders in the community prayed for new members for whatever they saw as bondage hindering their walk with the Lord. I remember seeking freedom from a heavy spirit that often oppressed me in times of prayer or teaching, freedom from rebellion, fear, and a kind of irrational anger that plagued some of my relationships. We learned in a deeper way that we need to take our own authority on the powers that oppress our surroundings, obsess our thinking, or depress our feelings. There is no reason why we need to live with bitterness, hatred, unforgiveness, gossip, compulsive eating, self-pity.

At the end of my stay in Ann Arbor I underwent another wave of personal teaching and experience as the three of us Sisters, part of the Kennedy household, were ministered to by Eileen Connolly, a three-week guest from the Darien, Connecticut, prayer group.

I've always been open to more—more teaching, more light, more freedom, more power—and into our parlor came more deliverance.

"Spirit of contention, I take authority over you in the

name of Jesus! In Jesus name you must go!"

It went . . . in the following days so did God deal with a rooted rebellion, frustration, condemnation, intolerance, judgment, rejection, stubbornness, grief, a gripping spirit of death, and occult bondage. We forgave and were forgiven. Along with the regular Ephesian armor for the battle I found myself for the first time in my life led to a week of complete fast except for liquids. Amazing grace! I suffered not one hunger pang or weakness, I had only growing, deepening joy, power, and victory.

In September I became one of the members of the H.O.P.E. (House of Prayer Experience) core group and a new life began. Both a new life and a new death, for it meant a heroic shifting of spiritual gears. It meant getting on the Potter's wheel again, allowing a new wholeness to come from a new brokenness. It meant being willing to die like the grain of wheat in the parable that out of death might come new life.

In prayer one day the Lord spoke prophetically of what was happening to all of us: "Like so many grains of wheat you have allowed yourselves to die, to be crushed, broken, ground into flour, and kneaded into one loaf to be fed to the multitudes."

Multitudes came to us at H.O.P.E. from the homes, convents, rectories, and prayer groups of New York and New Jersey. Within three years thousands of people came from every state, from Latin America, Canada, Australia, India, Thailand, Korea, France, Belgium, Austria, and Italy.

More than that, the House of Prayer Extension went out in teams to give renewal days, weekends, workshops, lectures, and parish and county-wide weeks of prayer. During my stay the community numbered eight weekend and thirty full-time members—five priests, one layman, four lay-women, and twenty-eight Sisters representing thirteen congregations or religious orders. Our community life was radically deeper than any experience we had ever had.

It was strongly supportive as well as challenging and demanding. Personality flaws that strained human relationships were brought into light, acknowledged, and entrusted to the healing power of the Lord.

In the process there was much effected in me also through the sacrament of reconciliation that could be classed under further inner healing and deliverance. The old powers threatened to close in. Early in my stay I recall sharing with my director one day: "If I would allow myself to think my 'unthunk' thoughts and to feel my unfelt feelings, they would spell rebellion in capital letters."

None of us die easily. Enablement—I guess this was what deliverance did for me more than anything else. It enabled me to be creative in encouraging a whole new realm of thought and feeling. Mountaintops or valleys made less and less difference until the day I was told, "Sister Fran, I believe God is calling you to return at this time to your Motherhouse." Never before in my life had I come to love a people, a place, and a work for the kingdom as I had come to love the House of Prayer. Never before in my life did I hear words to which I wanted to shout in response, "I will not. I cannot. God, You would not . . .!"

And yet once I had conquered the shock, the fear, the rebellion, I knew beyond the shadow of a doubt that it was right . . . .

My spiritual director slipped this word to me for my plane meditation: "You are on your way to the surrender of complete obedience to God's will through your superiors. What a gift! What a mellowing surrender and peaceful acceptance of your whole being, without fighting back or asserting your own will. Your whole life has led to this supreme moment of decision to give yourself helplessly yet definitely to God . . . self-righteousness goes . . . you are definitely being prepared to do whatever God is now preparing you for."

God led me out of that Promised Land into a year of desert experience—not for nothing, but for nothing but God.

From Jesus, the desert man *par excellence*, I learned a desert spirituality . . . the need to constantly turn with a loving trust to my Father and to forget everything but His love and His care. I found myself constantly "throwing in the towel" and saying, "Do it, God, do it." Not only did God do it, he had me doing it. For the first time in years I was asked by my superiors to take on a steady morning job that required no degrees. An old pride took on some new wounding! I found it hard to believe that God was calling me back to our Motherhouse to man the scrub bucket, mops, dust cloths, cleansers, and cleanups for our retired, aging, and infirm Sisters. For months in the morning I cleaned, during the noon hour I recuperated, and during the afternoon and evening I took to prayer and writing.

As early as January of 1972 God had been speaking to me through others about writing. At a conference in Anderson, Indiana, Frances and Charles Hunter shared one evening, "Sister Francis, the Lord is telling us to tell you to write a book. You begin by having someone type tapes of your talks."

Several months later when I had forgotten God reminded me through Katherine Beaman. "Sister Fran, you ought to write a book and when you do I'll type your tapes."

My amusement grew when several months later I began some Basic Behavior research for Ted Kennedy. He echoed, "Sister Fran, you ought to write a book." I explained about Frances and Katherine; we laughed and Ted added, "When Kate types she can use our tape recorder with the foot pedal."

The tapes rolled in and the pages rolled off. I stacked them away thinking "some day."

In late November of 1973, the "some day" came while I was in prayer at Convent Station, New Jersey. The Lord brought before me the scatter of papers like Ezekiel's valley of dry bones. Could these pages live?

I knew that I needed to pray it through . . . in tongues . . . for about an hour as I walked among the oaks, the cedars, and the maples. Finished, I understood in the Spirit what I could not understand in the flesh—how to put flesh on those dry bones.

Through it all God did a work in me.

Recently, my travels took me to a convent of Spirit-filled nuns in Marinette, Wisconsin, where I was called both to minister to and to be ministered to by Sisters Pat and Phyllis and Father Bert.

The story of my inner healing and deliverance would not be complete without sharing a special hour of grace during which the three ministered to me. It was then I experienced another round of inner healing and deliverance of many old areas that had become reinfected with self-pity, rejection, fear, new attitudes of an old rebellion, darkness, the whole family of griefs, and the spirit of death I had known in previous deliverances. After they prayed Pat diagramed around the main roots: tragic death and rejection, all I had come to know as bondage in my life. Looking at the charts it was hard to believe that any one person could suffer that much in one lifetime in the subconscious and still know the joy, the peace, and the love of the Spirit that I have known. I recalled a favorite line from Gibran's *The Prophet,* "Only as we are carved out by sorrow can we contain joy."

Next to the great mysteries of the Trinity, the death and the resurrection of Jesus, there is the eternal mystery of our own deaths and resurrections.

Someone shared recently that in his frustration to understand the mystery of God, God spoke to him: "If you would take your eyes off the mystery and put them on Me, you would come to understand the mystery."

Remember that I love all My people. There is none whom I despise. My heart longs for them all. There are none to be despaired of. You must work among them. Never allow your feelings to come in the way. I have put goodness in each one. You must draw it out; you must be kind, patient, and compassionate and you will make goodness flourish in others.

I have unleashed the Spirit upon the world and men's hearts will be converted — but freely. I force no one. The world is Mine. Never despair of it. Remember I am the Lord God and there is no Power equal to Mine. There is no force I cannot overcome. I am upon the earth and the earth is being made new.

You must be Apostles of the assurance of My love. You must be joyful and hopeful with your eyes ever turned toward Me, knowing that I am in the world and working in it. I give My love to each of you. I have you by the hand.

Chapter Sixteen
I Was in Prison

During my time at the Word of God community, the Lord opened a major adventure in evangelism at the Federal Correctional Institution in Milan, Michigan. It was July of 1972 when Father Granger, the Spirit-filled chaplain, invited Sister Lucienne and me to share in a Saturday afternoon ministry. The prison incarcerated about 650 men between the ages of eighteen and twenty-eight who were sentenced for everything from murder to smuggling heroin from Vietnam. Father was engaged in a six-day-a-week counseling program for the men and was interested to see what would happen if some of this Pentecost power broke loose in the Saturday afternoon meetings up in his chapel area.

I was immediately enthused for I was already conditioned to what God could do for prisoners from my visits to the Ann Arbor city jail. With this more stable population, much more could happen with permanent follow-ups.

The words of Isaiah the prophet had long been a favorite: "He has anointed me to bring good news to the afflicted; he has sent me to bind up the broken-hearted, to proclaim liberty to captives, and freedom to prisoners" (61:1).

I also found the perfect rationale for this new venture in the introduction to our new SSND Constitution, *You Are Sent:*

"to extend Christ in time and place as you willingly risk all things to help others believe that Jesus loves them and that their Father cares for them. To be Christ's body and blood, to be His hands and feet . . . to dare to dream the impossible dream that will bring hope to every person you meet."

From God we heard in prophecy: "Your only trouble might be to believe what I am ready to do or to take any of the credit."

No matter how "with it" we felt, we never ventured forth to prison without spending at least an hour together praising God and waiting for His direction. We aimed to go out in the spirit of "hanging loose with Jesus."

In this spirit He used us. I can still recall a bit of the trepidation on the first day when we were halted on our way from the parking lot by a voice from the lookout tower. "What's your business?" it boomed.

"We're from the church. We bring the Good News."

"Any alcoholic beverages, ammunition, camera, tape recorders, weapons, or explosives?"

"No, sir." As we became more familiar we'd add, "Nothing explosive but the love of God!" And we would get the word, "Pass on."

We passed on through the front business office charged with the acitivity of officers who were manning a room-sized, safety glass enclosed switchboard and key control. We sensed the friendliness of the officer as he signed us in as "church people," pushed a button for the iron-barred doors to roll back, and admitted us into a courtyard.

It was Saturday, so the place was peppered with prisoners free to make their choice of activities for the afternoon. Some took to playing basketball; a few sat on the grass in Lotu position, meditating; others chose to move with us across the yard and ascend the rather dingy back stairs to the chaplain's quarters.

In no time we had a sprinkling of men from every type of background: the atheist, the fallen away, the skeptic, the cynic. Usually we spent some time listening, visiting, and learning names to go with new faces before we suggested a bit of time for prayer and singing. Sister Marge would bring her guitar and sometimes some of the men brought theirs. It always surprised us how a few Christian songs could set the mood for prayer and the feeling of the presence of God in this otherwise godless place.

It also surprised us how God was ready to meet the needs of many of the men. I remember the first time we were there. One of the men asked for prayer for surgery he was about to have on his knees—it was a case of severely torn ligaments.

"God can heal you," we found ourselves boldly declaring. We were right, for as Sister Lucienne and I boldly reached out, John felt the power of God like an electric vibrator pouring a strong current of heat through our hands into his knees.

A week later John testified that he had checked with the doctor and there was no need for surgery, for the ligaments were completely healed.

The Good News spread: God is doing some amazing things. More and more men came to see for themselves. One day one of the fellows, rather chagrined, mentioned that he had a terrible case of VD that the doctors despaired of. I remember having second thoughts on whether we should ask God to heal this. After all . . .

Then I realized a need for repentance—mine.

The next week Joe witnessed, "The doctors have verified that I am completely healed of VD. Praise God!" I

139

am sorry I did not think to get the doctor's written statements on all of these healings. At the time God was doing so much that all we could take time to do was to let Him do some more!

Some Saturdays it seemed that God's healing power was there for special kinds of needs such as spine injuries or crippled conditions. As we prayed, God proved Himself the Divine Chiropracter. Nothing was too difficult or too complicated; adjustments were made in a matter of seconds.

All we would do was to check out the need (to see for ourselves that one leg was anywhere from one half to one and one half inches shorter). Then we would rest the legs on someone's palms, praise a bit, claim a bit, and many saw and felt for the first time the power of God working a miracle of His love in their bodies. Many felt a definite pulling in the leg and then they actually saw it move forward. Someone who had his eyes closed as the prayer was said cried out as he felt the tug, "Hey, you are pulling my leg." But there was no one touching him—no one except Jesus.

The only time the prayer did not work immediately was when there was an area of unforgiveness or resentment in the person who desired the healing. Once that was cleared, God's healing took effect. Sometimes we would have the last person who was healed say the prayer for the next one. As we did this one day, we met with a little fellow complaining, "But I ain't never said a prayer out loud in my life."

"Just say anything that is on your heart," we encouraged.

With that, Bob gulped. "Lord, what You did for me You can do for my brother." And that brother's leg literally shot out an inch to the length of the other.

In the year we ministered in the prison I can't recall one physical healing prayed for that God did not grant in some real way. I say in a real way, for when an operation was not called off, God did an incredible work through the doctors.

John needed a complicated stomach operation, for which we prayed. When we visited John in the hospital, John was chipper, dashing around, and feeling great. In the bed next to him was another fellow who had had the same operation the same day by the same doctor. He was in intense pain as well as in need of another surgery as soon as he recovered enough to take it.

Bob, president of the prison Alcoholic Anonymous, had a record of being arrested seventy times in the last seven years as an alcoholic. With a charm that must have served him in other situations, yet the picture of the prodigal beggar, Bob came to me asking for prayer for the healing of his ulcer. He had heard how God had healed his friend, Dave.

As we prayed up there in the prison chapel, Bob experienced first a gentle warmth, then a burning heat penetrating the whole area of affliction. When his physical healing was confirmed as complete, Bob came to ask how he might know Jesus as His Baptizer in the Holy Spirit.

We encouraged Bob to spend some time deepening his hunger, his thirst, and His expectation. We prayed for a complete healing of all the memories and circumstances that led to his life of degradation. Finally we prayed for his baptism in the Holy Spirit. Into this vessel that had known, as he shared with us, every possible degradation, despair, and bondage, God poured the fullness of love, of peace, of goodness, of wisdom, and of power. As he reeled under a heavy anointing he pealed forth God's praises in a new tongue. Bob knew another drunkenness—Jerusalem style—in the Holy Spirit. A drunkenness that led him to be literally bolted off his chair at the next AA meeting to give a witness of his life. This was something Bob had never had either the power or the desire to do. Once anointed with the boldness of the new Pentecost, Bob knew another boldness. Several times a week he gathered a group of Spirit-filled men in the chapel area to pray in other tongues.

In our prison prayer meetings the Lord often spoke the prophetic word in prison idiom, such as, "I'm going to get you one by one, so you might as well as surrender now!"

This was just the way it was happening—one by one. To everyone's amazement, one day it was Mike's turn. Mike was a small guy with one earring and a very controlled look.

"Sister, I'd really like to have Jesus in my life. My life has been one grand mess of sin . . ." (Even in the prison he headed a gang of seventy-five.) In a true spirit of repentance without boastfulness, Mike launched off material for a best-selling novel of sin and crime: adultery, drinking, dope peddling, smuggling, robbery. As a Satanist he had burned down four churches.

What a change even in his physical appearance from the shifty, mocking, frightened, flint-like eyes to the quiet, free, clear, blue light that now shone forth. As Sister led Mike in the sinner's prayer, the destruction of sin lifted and not only Mike's eyes but his skin took on the glow of a free man. (I've often wished that I might have had a camera with me to take the pictures of before and after. What a book these would make!)

If there is more joy in heaven over one sinner repenting, the same is true on earth. We rejoiced and praised God for every prodigal returned. To witness their catching the fire for others constantly amazed us! The Saturday following Mike's experience he was back glowing but burdened for his twin brother whom he had led into Satanism. He shared, "My twin brother has a tumor on the brain which he will not allow any doctor to touch, and he doesn't know Jesus. So would you pray for me in proxy for my brother that God will destroy that tumor and so that he will come to know Jesus."

Man, I thought, you've got more faith than I have. But if you have the faith, God has the power. We prayed.

The next week Mike reported, "I had a letter from my twin brother. He said the doctors cannot understand it but the tumor has completely disappeared."

Willie Norman, a beautiful black Chicago Catholic, approached me one day to ask if I would take him out on a church trip. Willie was due to be released in a month, but before his release, he wanted more than anything to go to a church where he could be part of a Mass again. He wanted to be in a home where he could talk and share.

The prison had a program that allowed for church trips for men about to be released if someone from the community would offer his services to accompany them and account for the seven hours they were permitted out. This was our first adventure with prison guests and so we did not quite know what to expect.

What happened was beyond our wildest dreamings, but not beyond God's. During his seven-hour leave, Willie accompanied us to the one P.M. Mass where God began a work. Only back home on Broadway did we realize what. Willie began sharing some of his background as a professional baseball player for the American League. Born into a family of blind parents, Willie was adopted into a wealthy family where he was offered opportunity to get ahead.

Get ahead he did! Yet always with a heaviness, a buried bitterness, and an unspoken resentment that he was not where he belonged. Complications grew. He made his way through the service, a marriage that brought unhappiness,

143

a career that ended in disaster, and now the prison for two years. "If only I could get rid of all the hurt . . ."

In awe we assured, "Willie, today is your day. God sent you here."

"All my life I have wondered about those stories of people really getting to know Jesus. More than anything, I really want Jesus in my life."

"Willie, today you will know that you know."

We shared with Willie in some detail how to accept Jesus, how to claim an inner healing, and then how to ask Jesus for the baptism in the Holy Spirit.

As we knelt we felt ourselves at the throne of the Father with Willie exclaiming, "I'm clean! I'm clean! It's like I never committed a sin in my life."

In that presence we prayed for the inner healing and the baptism of the Holy Spirit, in the midst of which Willie broke through with, "It's like a volcano just exploded inside of me!"

Later that afternoon Willie did something he had never done in his life: he gave a public witness to the work of Jesus in his life at our Word of God prayer meeting. About seven that evening we returned a new Willie to the prison, one who had lost the prison within. Willie shared: "This is the first time I have hope for a really new life for I am not going out alone." The several times I have heard from Willie confirms: "For I am confident of this very thing, that He who began a good work in you will perfect it until the day of Christ Jesus" (Philippians 1:6).

As in life, so in the prison—you win some and you lose some. Willie was typical of a "win"—Twig of a "lose."

Twig's nickname fit his frame—tall, lanky, somewhat gaunt yet handsome even in his prison khakis. Of all the men who were faithful to the Saturday gatherings perhaps Twig was the most faithful, most helpful, and most appreciated. Not only had he merited our trust and respect but that of the prison officials.

And so when Twig asked for a church trip, it was an easy yes from the officials and from us.

Attending a service, listening to remarks, enjoying a lunch, sharing his life, praying for a new start—Twig was both a blessing and blessed by his stay in Christian community until the hour for the return. With the suddenness of a flash of lightning, we realized Twig had disappeared. We prayed. We searched. We asked everyone who might have a lead. Finally we phoned the prison. "Twig disappeared about an hour ago. What do we do now?"

"It happens to the best of folks. No problem. We alert the FBI. And thanks again for helping us."

Two months later a repentant, humbled, chastened Twig was returned to Milan to pay the price for a moment's impulse.

The next Saturday Twig shared: "I was really relieved when they caught me for there is no peace in running from God, running from justice, or running from oneself."

I have brought you together here for My own purposes and you have been submissive to My will. Remember what I have said: I will use you when I will. There will be big moments and little moments — and no moments. The power is Mine. You have been faithful instruments.

I know how delicate you are. But I am the Master Craftsman and I know how to care for My instruments. I will keep you repaired. I will not cast you aside if you become broken. But I will repair you like new. Only lie smoothly in My hand. Do not try to do your own work; you are not capable of it. But if you lie smoothly in My hand, what wonders can I not perform, what beauties, what works of art, what consolations!

I love my people. I am always concerned for them. Do you not think I am aware of the evil in the world? Do you think I do not see those poor people — starving, unclothed, degraded? Do you think My heart does not bleed for them? But what can I do? I have made men free and I will not take back that freedom. I will work in My own way and it will be gently and it will be through you.

Chapter Seventeen
The Prisoner

"Any of you men want prayers today?"

That was the usual question we asked the unusual gang of guys in their prison khakis who gathered with Sisters Lucienne and Marge and me every Saturday afternoon in the chapel area of the Milan Federal Correctional Institution.

"Yeah, I could hardly wait until you guys got here today. I'd like to get rid of my hate," said a new guy with features mostly lost in a combined look of gloom, fear and hopelessness. His despairing blue eyes caught mine for a glimmer of hope when I said, "Sure, we'll pray. God is bigger than any hate!"

Encouraged, he went on, "I've been in prison since I was thirteen and I'm now twenty-three. Every time I get out for a couple months, there is a compelling hate that drives me to do something else, and I find myself right back."

"Yeah, and you can pray for Dave's ulcer, too!" a friendly buddy threw in.

We learned later that Dave's ulcerous condition had been so critical that he was doomed to take a whole bottle of Maalox every day, even on a bland diet. His medical records showed recent transfusions of seventeen pints of blood. The doctor's report that morning was, "I'm sorry, Dave, but your stomach is one ulcerated mess and there is nothing more that doctors or medicine can do. You'll just have to live with it."

We didn't know all this when we were asked to pray. All we knew was the word of another Physician of whom it was said through the prophet Isaiah: "He Himself took our infirmities, and carried away our diseases" (53:4). We knew assurance. "He gave them authority over unclean spirits, to cast them out, and to heal every kind of sickness" (Matthew 10:1). And Jesus' farewell words in Mark: "And these signs will accompany those who have believed: in My Name . . . they will lay their hands on the sick, and they will recover" (Mark 16:17,18).

We really believed those words, so we found ourselves responding to the double challenge of the hate and the ulcer without doubt or without hesitation. "God is bigger than any hate, and God is bigger than any ulcer! God is in the miracle business and so let's ask Him for a double right now!"

The three of us Sisters joined hands with about twenty prisoners and Norman and Rachel Schottin as we prayed, "Lord Jesus, we believe that You are present here as our Savior and our Healer. We praise and thank You for Your great love for all of us and especially for Dave. We praise You for all the circumstances of Dave's life that led to this condition of hate and ulcer. In the power of Your Name and the power of Your Blood we come against this hate in our brother, Dave. We command it to lose its hold; we bind it, cast it out, and put it under the power of Jesus. We claim an anointing of your love, Jesus, to fill every place where that hate was. We thank You, Jesus, that You are doing this right now."

For just a few minutes we freely prayed in English and in tongues. As we did, God's presence was sensed in the quiet and relaxed looks on the men's faces, a moment before tense with fear and hard without hope.

There was more to claim. "Jesus, You are not only the Savior or our souls but the Healer of our bodies. We claim Your healing love and Your healing light to enter Dave's body right now to destroy that ulcer. Touch him, Lord, with the fullness of Your resurrection power in every cell of his body, destroy all that needs to be destroyed and re-create all that needs to be recreated. We believe Your word that says: 'Where two or three are gathered and you ask for anything in My Name, it will be done.' We have asked in Your Name and we thank You that it is done. We accept this healing in whatever way You are giving it for the glory of the Father. Amen."

Our prayers were much like this—simply believing the power of His word. Later that day I prayed with Dave to accept Jesus as his personal Savior, and I prayed for an inner healing of all that led to his hate and the ulcer.

On our return the next Saturday, Dave met us at the outer gate—radiant, with a genuine smile, and the peace of Jesus written all over his features. "When someone becomes a Christian he becomes a brand new person inside. He is not the same anymore. A new life has begun!" (2 Corinthians 5:17, TLB).

Effervescing joy, Dave could hardly wait to pour out his story to our prison prayer group. "I just gotta thank God and all you guys for what He did for me this last week. You know, God really heard your prayers! I haven't got an ounce of hate left in me. I have only got love! The prison walls have disappeared. I know that they are there physically, but they are not there for me, for I'm free inside. This time when I get out, I know that I'm going to make it, for I am free within!

"And that ulcer! Man, there's not a trace left of it! When God heals, He heals good! I haven't had a pain since last

149

Saturday and I haven't taken a spoonful of medicine since. Sunday morning I had sausage and bacon for breakfast and pizza for lunch! What is even greater, I have begun praising God and I can't stop!"

A few weeks after his healing, I asked Dave to write a few memos of his background, his experience in coming to know Jesus, His healing, and whatever else he might want to share. This is Dave's story just as he wrote it from his prison cell November 16, 1972:

"In 1949, November 10, I was born in a little town in upper Wisconsin called Marinette. Shortly after I was born my mother and father moved from Marinette to Coleman, Wisconsin. When I was three years old, my parents again moved from Coleman to Fox Lake, Wisconsin, where we settled for eighteen years.

"After I had lived in Fox Lake for eight years, things began to happen. I started stealing cars and taking them for joy rides. Soon after I started that, I was caught and ended up in jail for the first time in my life. I thought that was a real joke because they released me the next day to my parents. Stealing cars just wasn't enough for me. I had to do more, so I started robbing stores around town; that lasted for a couple of months and I was busted again and again. I was taken to jail. This time they brought me in court and before a judge. He placed me on probation for six months, and then I was again released to my parents. I stayed out of trouble for five months but something drove me back to my old ways. I didn't know it then but I do now. It was the devil's work that drove me back to my old ways after five months.

"This time me and a friend robbed a store and were caught. I was held in jail for three weeks and finally went on trial in youth court. The judge found me guilty and sent me to the Wisconsin School for Boys at the ripe age of thir-

150

teen. I was there for four and a half years and finally was released at the age of seventeen and a half. I came back to my home town to start all over again. I was out two months and again I robbed another store. This time I was sentenced to three years at the Green Bay Reformatory. Now I thought I was really into the big time, but soon found out how hard life could really be. While I was serving those three years, I said to myself, I am going to have to change or I know I am going to spend the rest of my life in prison. I was released from prison on January 23, 1970. I stayed pretty cool for about six months and during that time I married. That was when all my problems started again.

"Four months after I was married I started forging checks. I received a year in jail and two years probation. My wife was due to have a baby in April and here I was sitting in jail! I was released from jail in six months because I did a good job. I moved my wife and son to Milwaukee, Wisconsin. That only lasted three weeks and she went home. I was really down in the dumps then; I was out of money; the rent was due. I really didn't know where to turn. I borrowed some money from my brother and bought a gun. I said to myself, 'I will get some money.' So on November 8, 1971, I robbed a bank at Fairwater, Wisconsin. They caught me and the judge placed me on five years' probation. That only lasted two and a half months and I forged some payroll checks. I was taken back into court and the judge revoked my probation and sentenced me to three years in prison.

"When I first came here to this prison, all I could do was hang my head and try to get up enough courage to kill myself. That went on for two weeks and finally one of my friends told me about the people of God who come to the chapel to pray for lost souls such as mine was. At first, I couldn't believe it, so I figured I would go and see for myself what was going on. The following week I went back again and I had those people pray over me. And from then on, my life has changed so much I could hardly believe it. I had those people pray for me so that God would take away my hate and bitterness and also to ask God to heal my ulcers. My friends, here is what happened: God not only healed my ulcers but he took away my hate and bitterness. He has changed my way of thinking from insane to sane. God has saved me from spending the rest of my life in prison. For so many years I hated my father. I no longer hate him, I love him!

"Before I came to prison I had bleeding ulcers, and when I came to the chapel, I had those people pray over me and just like that, my stomach felt better. The doctor had told me I would never again eat any pizza or spicy food. I eat it every day with no effect on my stomach. I was taking a bottle of medicine a day, and since I was prayed over, I don't have to take any medicine. God has saved me from spending the rest of my life in prison for the simple reason He has taken away my crime thoughts and restored my mind with love and kindness. My friends, I talk to God every day and He also talks to me. God helps me with my work and many other things. I thank God every day for what He has done for me. As it has happened to me, it will also happen to you if you will turn your life over to God. My friends, it is so great!"

. . . My daughters, put your trust in Me. Do not be discouraged. I see much more than you see. I can see that your trust in Me is growing. As you trust in Me, I will be able to release more and more of My power. I will be able to release more and more faith as you trust in Me. Do not be fearful. I have told you before that I am the Way. Just as this retreat group is being called to a healing of the nations, you are called to a healing of the wounds of religious.

Chapter Eighteen
S.F.P.S.

It had always been a matter of concern, curiosity, and sometimes amusement to me how Sisters come into the experience of the baptism of the Holy Spirit. For some time I was the only Sister in our convent of forty that was baptized in the Holy Spirit.

Then one day the Lord led me to share my experience with Sister Ethel. Her response was typical—"I'm too busy. Some day . . ."

A few weeks later the "some day" was there. I had invited Jim McInnes and Bill Bullard, who were Jesus People, to first share a school assembly and then an evening meal in our convent on Mulberry. Sister Ethel really had no desire to become involved but noting the lack of interest on the part of the other thirty-eight, she set herself to have dinner with them, to ask questions, and to accept an invitation to be present at their college sharing that evening.

The following night became known as "the night of the upper room," for we met with a crowd of interested college and high school students at Laughlin's. After listening to a "mind-blowing" tape on how the Mennonites in upper Minnesota received the Holy Spirit, thirteen teens and young adults packed into an upper room for prayer for the baptism of the Holy Spirit. In no time these thirteen had received the baptism with the manifestation of tongues. Glory! Bill had been drunk when he arrived but as he listened he truly sobered up. Weeks later Bill shared this testimony: "Drunk in the Spirit, I began praising God and I haven't ceased praising Him since."

After all of the young folks got blessed, I went down stairs to draw up some of the old folk. "Wouldn't you like prayers?" I asked Sister Ethel.

"I guess it wouldn't hurt me," was as enthusiastic a response as she could give. With that Sister came up, the whole group prayed but despite all the prayer and enthusiasm, the only tongues Sister Ethel could manage was, "I'm just an old dud. Let's go home." And so the "old dud" went home. She really went home a "new dud" although it took almost another twenty-four hours to realize it.

At a prayer meeting the following Friday Sister shared what really happened. "Toward evening I found myself in our chapel saying to God: 'Something has happened. I have never been able to pray like today. Now let's have the records straight. God, did I or didn't I receive the baptism in the Holy Spirit?'"

"I went on to say: 'God, if it means more suffering, I'm not sure I really want it. I have had enough of that in my life!'"

Then the thought came—sometimes if you swallow medicine fast, it doesn't taste so badly but it leaves you feeling better. At this time Sister found herself suddenly moved to say the stations meditating on the sufferings of Jesus. (In our chapels we have fourteen pictures or stations representing the sufferings of Jesus on the way to Calvary.) At each station one simple prayer flashed through her mind: "Sock it to me, Jesus!" And she prayed it with a fervor that did not come from *Laugh-In,* for she never watched that show.

Minutes later God "socked it to her." When she got to her bedroom and opened her mouth intending to say some prayers in English, they came forth in a torrent of tongues . . . in a beautiful unknown language.

Startled because she knew little if anything about this, Sister opened the book *This Awakening Generation* by John Osteen. In a bold print magnified just for this reading, were the words: "This awakening is from God!"

It was an awakening, and it was from God. With it came a new power to praise, a new desire to read the Word, and a new realization of the charisms of the Holy Spirit.

With this new power to praise, Sister saw the hopeless pieces of her sister's marriage come together. The family had been praying for this for seventeen years. It was such an amazing answer to prayer that even the priest who had been working on the case marveled: "Never have I seen such a preposterous moving of mountains!"

The desire to read the Word took on such power that Sister not only could but would spend days praying the Scriptures. Even Protestants began to say, "That Catholic Sister really knows her Bible."

In the past two years I have prayed with countless Sisters in their sixties, seventies, or eighties for the full release of the Holy Spirit they have known in part all of their lives.

Sister Mary Julia, my former Novice directress, after twenty years of service in Rome, received this new experience of prayer while hospitalized at Salvator Mundi Hospital in Rome. On Sister's return to the States in 1970 she began searching in earnest, reading with a passion, and finally exclaiming: "This is it! Let's get with it! What are we waiting for?"

Not only did Sister get with it, but she has stuck with it, and she has spread it with all the vehemence of her Irish wit, her Roman influence, and her nearly eighty years.

Sister Mary Philip was one of our Sisters in Marion Hall, confined to her bed, her rocker, and the books she read. *Like A Mighty Wind* was a book I knew Sister would enjoy, but I never dreamt it would speak to her as it did. On passing her room one day I said, "Sister, how did you enjoy the *Mighty Wind*?"

Here was a woman eighty years old and sixty years a Religious summing it up in these words: "That was the greatest book! I've got it all figured out. It is so simple! It is so simple! All you do is get to love Jesus. To really love Jesus! And then you ask Him to baptize you in the Holy Spirit."

"Did you do it?" was all I could say.

"I surely did."

"How did you know how?"

"It told you in the back of the book."

Sister M. Regis, in her late seventies, had been asking for books to read like *Prison to Praise, The Cross and the Switchblade,* and *They Speak With Other Tongues.* With each book the desire grew to have what they had. Finally we set a time to pray. Hardly had I touched her when I realized she was speeding away in a magnificent "other" tongue.

In the spring of 1970 while sharing a Nicky Cruz conference, I met Sister Conrad, a Benedictine from Eau Claire, Wisconsin. One day as Sister was driving home from work she was overwhelmed with the goodness of God. She began praising! All of a sudden it came out in these strange sounding syllables.

It sounded funny but it felt good. So she kept right on until she got home. Then she panicked. "What's happening to me?"

In the convent she remarked, "Sister Superior, I think I

need psychological help." Sister related what had happened to her.

"Oh you're just over-tired. You'll be all right in the morning," her Superior explained.

In the morning she was all right. It wasn't happening any more. And it didn't happen again until a month later. Sister found herself driving home and all these strange sounds and syllables were coming out. She thought, I do need psychological help, but I'll wait until summer.

In the meantime she noticed a list of retreats that were being given in the summer and one was headed "Charismatic," preached by Father Francis MacNutt. "That sounds kind of psychological. Maybe that will help," she thought.

In his first talk at the retreat Father related, "God is pouring out His Spirit upon people all over the world and people are praying in 'other' tongues."

Sister thought, Tongues? I wonder if that could happen if no one prayed with you?

"Tongues," Father said in the next sentence, "sometimes happens even when no one prays with you."

While on the Scandinavian-European airlift, eight of us stayed in Johannesgarden, a modern scenic Catholic Retreat Center sprung up in a one percent Catholic Sweden. It was run by the Sisters of the Sacred Heart. Some spoke English and so we loved sharing with them highlights of the meetings and services. Much was happening that we could see and describe and yet the Lord reminded us one night, "If you think you see something on the surface you should see what is happening underneath."

God had been preparing this "ground" for a long time. One Sister, eighty-four years old and fluent in seven languages, could not rest until she added one more. The

Sisters had wind of Pentecostal happenings in places like Notre Dame and Duquesne. "Was it true?" they asked.

We met and shared here with key clergymen such as the Bishop of Norway and the Vicar General of Sweden. I was amazed one day when Father Lee Hayer exclaimed: "Do you realize that your Sisters—the School Sisters of Notre Dame missioned out of Munich—are teachers in our parish here in Goteborg?" (Father was a California-born, Spirit-filled priest missioned to Sweden out of Germany.) "Could you come to the convent and share with them about the charismatic experience?"

We checked possible times. Due to the national holiday to welcome the coming of spring, May first was the only day we were without a full schedule of churches, colleges, and schools to go to. It was also the only day the Sisters were free to listen.

The meeting was set for 11 A.M. with Father Heyer as interpreter for English, Swedish, German, and tongues. Jesus bridged the cultural differences as they in the traditional long black garb, and I in a blue suit, chatted and exchanged. While I came to know them, their convent, and a typical Swedish dinner and snacks, they came to know something of the Charismatic Renewal in the U.S.A. It helped to have with me a copy of the *New Covenant* featuring "Sisters in Charismatic Renewal."

When it got to be three o'clock I asked, "If any of you Sisters would like prayer for physical healing we would be glad to pray with you."

"Physical healing, nothing. I would like this baptism of the Holy Spirit," one of the senior Sisters announced.

"No need to make a choice, you can have both," I assured.

Before I left at five they did receive both. They preferred that we take each Sister aside to pray privately for healing needs, but when it came to the baptism we prayed together for all nine. And together all nine received.

Before leaving they wanted to make sure that I would be able to share with our Sisters in Stockholm. "You've just got to share with our Notre Dame Sisters in Stockholm. It is the only other Notre Dame convent in the whole of Sweden."

"Would you believe it—Stockholm was the only other place I had planned to go," I said. "The last three days of the airlift all the 170 participating are meeting for a three-day international conference at the Amaranten Hotel."

Sister phoned ahead and I left Goteborg a day early to spend it at our Notre Dame convent in Stockholm. After an evening together and several chances to share the F.G.B.M.'s conference at the Amaranten, the Sisters invited our American Catholic group to their convent for an afternoon Mass, coffee, and prayer for the baptism of the Holy Spirit.

Here there was an interesting incident of nearly backsliding before in-sliding.

Before we were to arrive at the convent that day I phoned for final directions. With the directions, the Sister who spoke the best English spoke for the rest, "We decided we have enough of the Holy Spirit. We are not interested in the baptism. You can come for dinner but forget about the prayer."

My first reaction was disappointment. I wondered if we should even go.

After prayer we realized God wanted us to go in love and to trust. What happened was beyond our wildest scheming and our dreaming. With a larger group going, the Sisters could ask their questions on an almost one-to-one basis. We had a wonderful time at lunch. When it was time to leave, the oldest and jolliest Sister in the group said, *"You are not leaving* until I get this baptism in the Holy Spirit."

"Okay, we're not leaving until this Sister gets the baptism of the Holy Spirit," Father affirmed. "And if anyone else wants to watch how it happens come to the chapel with us."

Seven of them came and one after the other, seven of them received. As the last one received, the Lord gave a word of prophecy in tongues and interpretation for their convent: "I have had My eye on you for a long time. Indeed you are the apple of My eye. I am about to break the powers of darkness that rule this land and as I do I will make of you a light to the whole of Sweden. I will allow you to keep some of the old but I will give you much of the new."

Because of my own struggles, I have had a special burden for Sisters on the verge of leaving, for Sisters in need of inner healing, and for Sisters who need encouragement to ask for the baptism of the Holy Spirit.

There have been multiple examples of each. One who impressed me most was a Medical Missionary Sister studying to be a medical doctor. One day as we were sharing in our House of Prayer I discovered that she had been a former student of mine. Then it became clear that whatever it was we had she desperately wanted. Even though she went by a Religious name she agonized in the fact that for several years she had completely lost her faith. She could no longer believe as truth any of what we were expressing. The most she could do was sing our songs for she loved to sing.

Where all this was leading she had no idea. She was becoming more and more desperate for an answer. Years before I might not have known how to help her. Now it was as simple as asking, "Rosemary, do you know Jesus? Do you have a personal relationship with Jesus?"

"No, I am sure that I don't. But I would really like to. Would you pray with me?" It was as simple as that, not only to save her vocation, but to really empower her to live it. When she writes, it is a new Rosemary not entirely without problems, but with power to live with hope. And when she signs her letters, it is not just Sister Rosemary, M.D., but B.A. (Born Again) and S.F.P.S. (Spirit-Filled Precious Sister).

I know that you have been busy about My work. Now you must rest for a while. I would speak to you in silence; you must learn to listen to Me in silence. I can be a God of thunder but my preference is gentleness. I want to speak to you in quiet. I want to train your ear to listen to Me in silence.

Give glory to My Name and extoll My wonders. Every day of your life give glory to My Name and thanks to your God for the mighty deeds He has wrought. Look about you and see Me in every good thing. Look about you and see where I am not, and put Me there.

Chapter Nineteen
We Walk in Miracles

"God is amazed that we are amazed at the amazing things He does."

Father MacNutt, who figured prominently in the Notre Dame healing service writes in his book *Healing:*

"We are now seeing a return of the direct experience of God's healing power in such striking ways that the living tradition of the Church—what the Spirit is helping us to experience and understand today—is leading us again to a more lively awareness of what Jesus did in his healing ministry. If we ourselves see miracles of healing, we no longer have the difficulty of visualizing the healings in the gospels. Suddenly, everywhere I travel I discover that people are experiencing at firsthand the healing power of God."

Someone has said that, as we meet Jesus in the Gospels, it seems that either He is in the act of healing someone, He has just come back from healing someone, or He is about to heal someone.

In a workshop of Morton Kelsey's on "Healing" he left us something similar to ponder: "In the New Testament alone 729 verses deal with healing, either with the promise of healing or an example of healing. Now if you do not believe in healing, let's cut out all those Scriptures you do not believe in."

Mr. Kelsey had a Bible in which he had cut out all those Scriptures—729 of them. "Now here are your 'holey' Scriptures!" And indeed they were "holey" with a sixth of a page missing, a seventh, a fifth, a fourth!

"If you do not believe what is cut out, then why do you believe what is left?" he challenged.

How can we separate, divide, and condition God's Word? How can we separate the healing ministry from the saving ministry since He effected both by the same act? Jesus died to not only save our souls but to heal our bodies. Just as we were saved almost 2,000 years ago, we were also healed 2,000 years ago. The day we claim salvation, it is ours. And the day we claim healing, it is ours.

The thing that should surprise us is not that God is working miracles today but that He hasn't been working them all these hundreds of years because of our unbelief.

"When I came to this retreat my back was like an S. Now it is straight as an arrow! And that isn't all," Sister Mary said, "I knew when you prayed that something happened for I felt a penetrating heat. But when Sister Marie and I were kneeling in the back of the chapel after the prayer we both actually heard a clicking of the bones. There was no denying the sound. Click! Click! Click! All through that first night every time either of us awakened there was this audible clicking of vertebrae telling us God was doing a miracle.

"The next morning was the first time in forty years I was able to bend from the waist down. When I was a child of six, my back had been injured when I fell from a horse. Every chiropractor I have gone to had the same story. 'Sister your back is like an S.' Now they have the same comparison—straight as an arrow! Praise God!"

166

Along with praying for healing, I have found it important to share how to keep one's healing. I shared evening vespers with a community of Franciscan Sisters in Chicago. After the prayers I was moved to share a bit about healing and to offer prayers for anyone with a need.

One of the Sisters had never been able to breathe through her nostrils. After prayers, Sister discovered she could breathe wonderfully well and that she could call off a pending surgery. Three of the Sisters had back ailments to the extent that they could not sleep at night without medication. Before we prayed I warned, "The enemy may be around creating symptoms even after God has touched you. The thing to do is to take authority of the symptoms: 'Pain, I command you to leave in the name of Jesus! Jesus, I claim Your healing power!' "

The warning was well given. Two of the Sisters were healed immediately. The other had worse pain than ever that night until she took authority over the pain.

We can't really make rules. Someone asked Kathryn Kuhlman to write a book on the theology of healing. She said, "I can't, because God keeps changing it. I used to think you had to be a believer yourself to receive a healing until the day God healed an atheist just looking on and gave him the faith afterwards."

What was true for the Sisters was different for a friend up in Battle Creek, Michigan. A guest at their home, Burdette asked for prayer for his back before he went to the Sunday morning service. There was no evidence of the healing until he stood up in his church and testified, "I had a strange thing happen to me today. I had a Catholic Sister pray with me for the healing of my back. I believe God healed me." As he said these last words the pain left and has never returned.

Sometimes we think things are too little or too insignificant to ask God to heal. One night at our dinner

167

table Noel happened to mention that she had been allergic to chocolate for more years than she could remember. It was something she thought she would have to live with for the rest of her life. God had other thoughts. After we prayed Noel ate her first Hershey in years. But not the last. To this day she has been enjoying chocolate with no ill effects.

Father Woodford shared recently with our group that when some of us insisted on praying for his phlebitis condition he almost rebelled against our ministry. He thought with all the people in the world suffering much greater afflictions he should be able to suffer this lesser affliction. That night as he was driving home the Lord spoke to him. "Do you think that just because I would heal your phlebitis I would not have enough power to go around to the rest of the world?"

"Go report to John what you have seen and heard: the blind receive sight, the lame walk, the lepers are cleansed . . . and blessed is he who keeps from stumbling over Me" (Luke 7:22,23). Thinking back of all the miracles I have seen and heard, the two that have touched me the most were the miracles of the blind seeing and a leper cleansed.

Along with us on the Scandinavian-European airlift was a miracle boy, Dave Pelletier. As a result of a fire-cracker accident in 1969 Dave lost the sight of one of his eyes. Today he not only sees with 20-20 tunnel vision through his glass eye, but he also reads through the empty socket.

I've witnessed this miracle together with thousands of others, including at least ten American and two Swedish ophthalmologists.

In demonstrating this miracle before a large international gathering, David's father asked for a Bible with small print. I passed my Living Bible. Nonchalantly, with the good eye covered, David opened my Bible and through his glass eye read Amos 9:1: "I saw the Lord standing beside the altar, saying, 'Smash the tops of the pillars and shake the temple until the pillars crumble and the roof crashes down upon the people below.'"

In my spirit, I understood this Word to say, "I am going to smash your unbelief. If I can create, I can recreate." David continued to demonstrate the mighty power of God. "Cutting" the Scriptures a second time he removed his glass eye and read from my Bible through the empty socket Acts 2:11,12: "And we all hear these men telling in our own languages about the mighty miracles of God. They stood there amazed and perplexed. 'What can this mean, they asked each other!'"

The next day the Swedish paper *The Dagen* carried the headlines, BOY SEES THROUGH GLASS EYE!

In the summer of 1973 I was at the Americana in New York when Rogelio Parillo, a man who was a leper for fourteen years gave the moving testimony of his healing. A leper since he was ten, Rogelio in a few years became the most repulsive-looking of all the lepers in the colony. So much so that his companions protested his presence in the common dining area. His voice was almost entirely eaten away so that he could no longer sing. His only hope was an early death until a group of Christian people came to the leper colony to conduct a service there.

Rogelio heard for the first time about Jesus saving, filling, and healing. There is hope even for me, he thought. After a long wait at the very end of a very long line, finally two hands were placed on his head as Pastor Torres said this prayer: "Spirit of leprosy, I cast you out in this man in the name of Christ Jesus!"

Returning to the colony that night Rogelio told the doctor there that he had been healed. The doctor said, "We must take tests to prove whether you are healed or not."

After many examinations, cross-examinations, and conferences Rogelio reports, "Everyone agreed and declared that I was a healed man."

Even Rogelio's voice was completely restored so it can be said that not only has one leper been cleansed but one more has returned to Jesus to sing his thanks.

I was at Notre Dame on June 15, 1974, the night of the historical first healing service for a Catholic charismatic convention. I was among the 40,000 standing in the rain, drenched, and deeply moved by the healing power of God that moved over that assembly.

"The Lord wants each one of us to believe He will heal *me*. As He leaves He wants to look back over Notre Dame, as He looked back over the towns He left, knowing He had healed every single person there . . . If you need healing from sin, if you are troubled in spirit, He desires to heal you. If you have anguish, any fear, any relationships, any sickness that doctors have given up on—He wants to heal you. Any money or job problems—He wants to heal now.

"The deepest healing many of us need is to know how much He loves us. Let us go out of the darkness and let Jesus, Light of the World, heal you!"

Many accounts have been written of that night with varying degrees of skepticism, belief, and unbelief. Attempts have been made to explain and to explain away what happened. The important thing is not the numbers healed or the kinds of diseases healed, but that as a people of God we were willing to let go of all that was darkness and to move into the marvelous Kingdom of Light.

The important thing was that 40,000 believers were

moving in the flow of the Spirit, aware that Jesus was present in that stadium as the Healing Light of the World. They were aware that Jesus was speaking to them through two women beautifully using the word of knowledge as they called out numerous diseases that were being healed at that very moment.

"We thank You, Father, for the gentleness of Jesus moving to heal chronic things—cancer . . . leukemia . . . arthritis, some of which has been so bad that you could not move. All pain is being taken in His Body so you can be free.

"Liver damage . . . problems contracted because of alcohol disease are being taken from the stadium. Stand firm in the faith that you are being made whole. Stand firm in the faith that God's power is rushing through your nervous system as you are being healed of neurological difficulties. Heart trouble . . . the Lord is being faithful to you because you were faithful to Him when the world said there was no hope.

"Victims of stroke—the parts paralyzed are beginning to open up. Through the controlling love of Jesus the parts you couldn't control are brought back to wholeness. Diseases of the stomach and intestines—problems doctors said would be cured only by surgery, problems you have taken medication for for years are being healed . . .

"Jesus is giving sight to the blind. Problems are being corrected. Feel the healing light penetrate. The haze is being obliterated. Things obscure are being made clear.

"Healings are coming so fast that no power in heaven or on earth can stop what is going on. Epileptics come under the healing power of God. As you feel a hand on your head know that the parts of your brain needing correction are being made whole as Jesus intended.

"People from prayer communities and burdens from home are being touched. Power is not limited to this place.

171

They are saying what is happening as they are being touched. A baby in the womb seven months with RH-factor blood type is being changed. There's a family of four with a blood disease—at this moment the blood is being changed."

The following sung first in tongues and then with interpretation speaks of why God should desire to heal with such marvelous extravagance: "I have mercy. I have mercy. I have wonderful mercy. I want to wash your feet. I want to heal you. I want to come into your heart. Open yourselves to Me. Open yourselves to Me and let Me come in. I want to heal you tonight. I have mercy on you."

Our God was never a God of statistics. John ends his Gospel with: "And there are also many other things which Jesus did; which if they were written in detail, I suppose that the world itself would not contain the books which were written" (21:25).

There will be no place in your ministry for harshness, or bitterness, or resentment, or judgment. I want you to be always kind, always gentle, always optimistic, always joyous, always alive with My life, always alight with the flame of My love.

Make it shine and make it warm for all who come in contact with you. Touch many hearts. I have taken possession of your heart. Now you must give me your mind. Do not contrive thoughts to figure out My plans. Do not question what I do. Do not debate within yourselves what is right and what is wrong. Be simple.

I will be with you moment by moment. Do not look for My message tomorrow in the today. Every day I have something new to tell you but it will be for today, for this moment. In this way I will lead you. In this way I would have you strengthen your trust in Me. Become like little children with their hand in the hand of their father. They go where He leads because they trust him. They do not know where they are going or why. They only know that He is their father and will bring them no harm.

Chapter Twenty
"East is East"

Since that night of my testimony, I have come to be very much at home in churches of all denominations. In fact, I am very much at home with non-Catholics in general, for I am a nun-Catholic . . .

In the past three years I have been invited to share in Protestant churches, schools, colleges, and youth groups. I have shared on Christian radio, video tapes, television, at Full Gospel Businessmen's conferences, and Women's Aglow groups, and in overseas evangelism. My first trial and run experiences were just that: trial and run.

I dare say we have all been indoctrinated with the same prejudices, filled with the same fears, controlled by the same hates. Your church and my church, your school and my school, your home and my home taught us not just to "play it cool" but to "play it hot." Long before Ireland took to staining her sod with denominational blood, we fought our wars with shouts, sticks, and stones from our side of the street, our side of the fence, our end of town. It was your ball team against ours—the Protestanters versus the Catlikkers. It was "East is East and West is West and ne'er the twain shall meet."

Then along came this man whom the world came to

know and love as "Papa John," Pope John. He began opening a lot of doors and windows that had been bolted for centuries. So did the rest of us! Dialoguing did not come easy but it came wherever minds were open and souls were searching.

I recall the summer of 1964 when I was studying for my Master's in guidance and counseling. In fun, I claimed to be carrying an extra course, "getting acquainted with everyone on the campus." (To understand this boldness, you would have to appreciate that at this time it was the custom at a summer school to mingle only with Sisters of your particular religious order.)

Strolling across the campus one day enroute to class, I happened to share my invented course title with a Protestant. "Sister, this is great! You know, you are the first Catholic nun I have ever talked to in my life." Tom proceeded to tell "what a great guy" he thought "John" was. But "this thing within the church, this brotherly love" he was experiencing on the Loras campus . . . he couldn't get over it. It was a first!

Since then there have been many firsts of Protestants coming to know Catholics and vice versa. Perhaps this is a first time many of you are reading a book by a Catholic nun. All I can say is, "Praise God you have come to this." A decade ago I would not have thought that I had a thing to say to non-Catholics, except perhaps to defend doctrine, sacrament power, or a dream that when all the world became Catholic, there would be "one flock and one Shepherd." All of us must have had variations of this same dream. And all the while God must have been smiling. For He was not saying that at all. What He was saying was that there would be one flock and one Shepherd when men would know Jesus as their personal Savior and true Shepherd.

I am thinking how God has changed all of us—not

asking us to compromise, not asking us to deny any of the truths we have known, but simply opening us to a vision of what we have been missing. Now there is more stress on the Word of God, more understanding of Revelation, more forgiveness of our sins, more joy in our salvation, more faith in the Name of Jesus, and more gifts of the Holy Spirit.

Once we all put more stress on the *who* we believe in rather than the *whats,* a lot of the whats that have separated us become so-whats. So what if you believe in (what do you believe in?) what I don't. So what if you believe in immersion and I believe in pouring. It is not so much how we get it as long as we are born again into the family of God, and who we walk with after we are in . . . and in what measure of God's power.

I am thinking of the time I shared a Scandinavian airlift with 170 Spirit-filled Christians of all denominations. If we had gone forth in the old tradition—if you want to be a Catholic, believe these things; if you want to be a Lutheran, believe these things—no one would have listened to anyone. But because we came asking, "Do you know Jesus?" "Are you a born-again Christian?" "Have you experienced the baptism in the Holy Spirit?" people listened. They were freed from the bondage of Satan; their bodies were healed; they were encouraged to attend again the church of their youth.

At a Christian fellowship dinner in Stockholm, a young man who had attempted suicide a couple of weeks before came asking, "Sister, would you pray with me that I might know Jesus in my life?" Not only did he come to know Jesus, but was also baptized in the Holy Spirit! That evening he came to the church service asking prayer for deliverance from bondage to drugs, alcohol, and the occult powers of darkness. As this last obsession lifted, he exclaimed, "Wait a minute, Sister." He reached into his pocket, put on his glasses, and discovered he no longer needed them. In the minute that his spiritual sight was restored, his physical vision was restored . . . without any special prayer for it.

The morning after our first sharing in Joteborg, a Swedish missionary, forty years in the missions, sixty-eight years old, phoned me at eight in the morning to ask if it were too late for her to receive the baptism of the Holy Spirit. "Too late, it's not yet nine o'clock in the morning!" By nine, the traditional hour of Pentecost, as the Catholic nun prayed, one more Lutheran was baptized in the Holy Spirit.

It has been a long time coming—the renewing, the remaking, and the restoring of God's people. How well I recall the first time I was startled out of my salvation complacency in the summer of 1970. It was my first attendance at a Full Gospel Businessmen's Convention in the Chicago Hilton. Peter Marshall, Jr., gave a stirring message that night on repentance. In the after-talk, Rev. Jarman came to me questioning, "Are you saved, Sister?"

I was startled. After forty-four years as a baptized Catholic and twenty-five years as a Catholic nun, I wondered how anyone might have dared to question me. Just then Peter came to my rescue, patted me on the back and encouraged, "That's all right, Sister. Stay just the way you are."

I praised God for Peter Marshall. But I also pondered Rev. Jarman's question, "Are you saved, Sister?" I came to understand: it was asked by a minister who had been preaching for fifty years without knowing Jesus Christ himself.

It is possible for a Sister or any other baptized person to be preaching Jesus and to know a lot about Jesus without knowing Jesus Christ Himself.

Billy Graham once remarked, "Churches of all

denominations have given their people a lot of doctrine to believe in and have just taken it for granted that their people have had an experience to go with it." The fact that many have not, accounts for many eventually losing whatever faith they did have. When other ideas, philosophies, or experiences call for a choice, it is comparatively simple to abandon one idea or philosophy for another. But to give up a relationship with Jesus would be something very different.

Perhaps the greatest shift all denominations need to make is that shift of emphasis from the *whats* we believe in to the *who* we believe in. It is in this common ground of the *who* we believe in that I have seen thousands of Christians of all denominational backgrounds worshiping together "in Spirit and in Truth." Did not Jesus prophesy concerning this when He said to the woman at the well, "But an hour is coming, and now is, when the true worshipers will worship the Father in Spirit and truth" (John 4:23).

What we have made so complicated can be so simple when we allow God to reveal Himself not only to our minds but also to our hearts. As some mathematician computed it, it is possible to miss heaven by seventeen inches—the distance between the mind and the heart, the difference between the *what* and the *who*.

That night in Chicago I came to understand something of the impact of our separation, the division, and the tragic way we have been taught to view one another. For centuries much of the non-Catholic world has been taught to label the Church of Rome as the harlot church of Ezekiel, the Whore of Babylon. So it is the most natural thing in the world for non-Catholics to have all those unholy thoughts about any possible holiness in the children of a harlot. It is

179

natural for them to question my relationship with Jesus Christ, my baptism in the Holy Spirit, and my adoption as a child of the Father.

We can only begin to understand the prejudices that have separated us, where we have been, and how far we have come, when we reminisce incidents such as the following.

A Full Gospel Businessman related to me that a few years ago the Lord gave him the interpretation for a prophecy that went much like this: "I will pour out My Spirit on all flesh: the Baptists, the Congregationalists, the Methodists, the Lutherans, the Presbyterians, the Anglicans, the Episcopalians, the Orthodox . . ." all the way down the line until he came to the Roman Catholics. He could not force himself to say it, it was so repulsive. So he blurted out, "And other denominations."

Several years ago in a Pentecostal church in St. Peter, Minnesota, I was sharing prayer for the healing of the pastor's little boy, Stevie. Stevie had never been able to walk on his heels for the tendons in the back of his legs were too short. That night we witnessed Isaiah 35:6: "The lame will leap like a deer."

For me, greater than the healing was the incident that followed. An old lady came to me that night took my hand and said, "Sister, when I saw you praying with the minister's son for healing, I wept tears of joy for the healing that is going on in the Body of Christ. This is much greater than any physical healing."

God is doing a sovereign work! We cannot program it. We cannot halt it. We can say, "Do it, God! Do it!" We can move when He says, "Move!" We can praise God for what we see happening!

If we have eyes to see and ears to hear, we have the evidence all around us that God is not only renewing and remaking, but restoring His people through all His churches. Sharing in some of the historic churches in Sweden, I was amazed to hear someone say, "This is the first time we have had a Catholic speak from our pulpit since the Middle Ages."

"But blessed are your eyes because they see, and your ears, because they hear. For truly I say to you, that many prophets and righteous men desired to see what you see, and did not see it; and to hear what you hear, and did not hear it" (Matthew 13:16,17).

In the course of the past three years, I have had opportunity to share with many great men across the country. John Osteen, a Spirit-filled Baptist minister, author and missionary, is one of them. John shared with me the burden the Lord has given him for the Catholic Church. One day as he was traveling, he had a vision while resting in the back seat of his car. He saw a mountain suddenly loom up; it began to tremor and to shake. Pieces began to roll down the front, down the back, and down the sides. As the pieces rolled and the mountain shook, gradually out of this mountain emerged the head of man, then the shoulders, and then the whole form of a man shot out of that mountain and disappeared into the sky.

God gave John to understand that this mountain was His Roman Catholic Church, which He would shake and shake and shake until out of this structure emerged the free man, freed to the glory of God.

In sharing the charismatic renewal, I have come against some of these mountains of prejudice. But I have heard the Lord speak in prophecy against them, "I will not be overcome by intellectual prejudice nor will I suffer my work to be stayed by religious prejudice. Who is to say that it is not My time to come forth in power? For I will come forth like a man drunken with power and I will shake the very pillars of your tradition." (Prophecy given by Kenneth Hagin after Father MacNutt's talk in Omaha.)

God is doing a new thing. Ralph Martin spoke of it at the 1974 International Conference on the Catholic Charismatic Renewal. "If we love the Catholic Church as it is so much that we won't let Jesus make it what He wants it to be for today, we become the enemy of the Catholic Church."

From the 1975 International Conference on Catholic Charismatic Renewal in Rome we heard the prophetic word of the Lord given in St. Peter's Basilica at the closing service. "See what I am doing in the world today. I am renewing My people. I will renew My church. I will make My people one. I want to prepare you for what is to come. Days of darkness are coming on the world, days of tribulation, days of trial, days when the supports that hold My people will no longer be there. Buildings that are now standing will not be standing. Supports that are there for My people will not be there . . . I will strip you of everything you are depending on now so that you will depend just on me. Be prepared and when you have nothing but Me, My people, then you will have everything—lands, fields, homes, brothers, sisters, love, joy, and peace more than ever before . . ."

At the same conference, following the main address in French, Pope Paul spoke informally to us in Italian. "Where the Spirit is concerned we are immediately alert, immediately happy to welcome the coming of the Holy Spirit. More than that, we invite Him, we pray to Him, we desire nothing more than that Christians, believing people should experience an awareness, a worship, a greater joy through the Spirit of God among us. Have we forgotten the Holy Spirit? Certainly not! We want Him, we honor Him, and we love Him, and we invoke Him. And you, with your devotion and fervor, you wish to live in the Spirit. This should be where your second name comes in—a renewal. It ought to rejuvenate the world, give it back a spirituality, a soul, and religious thought; it ought to reopen its closed lips to prayer and open its mouth to song, to joy, to hymns, and to witnessing. It will be very fortuitous for our times, for our brothers, that there should be a generation, your generation of young people, who shout out to the world the glory and the greatness of the God of Pentecost.

"And we will say only this: today, either one lives one's faith with devotion, depth, energy, and joy or that faith will die out."

It has shocked me sometimes that God's people can be blind, stubborn, prejudiced. Yet looking back into my own experience, I can say, "I understand."

And so I've come to you gently, not saying, "I've got something you haven't got," but saying, "I've got something I never had before." Not saying, "This is something you have to have," but that "You can have it if you want it." "For the promise is for you and your children and for all who are far off, as many as the Lord our God shall call to Himself" (Acts 2:39).

HOW TO EXPERIENCE THE BAPTISM IN THE HOLY SPIRIT

"Something is happening in America, some new sign of hope, some star in the darkness: you are not only rediscovering Jesus as Lord, you are also rediscovering that the Spirit of Jesus is alive today and working in your midst. The accentuation of the Holy Spirit in our times is certainly a sign of hope, but we need more than right thinking about the Holy Spirit: we need a renewed encounter with, a new surrender to, the Holy Spirit. I seriously believe that in this Charismatic renewal there is something very important for the renewal of the Church, something that will help us toward a real visible unity with God, I think that we have here one of the wonders of God today."

(Cardinal Leo Josef Suenens)

First of all never forget that Jesus is the Baptizer. Don't seek an experience but seek Jesus Christ and His Kingdom. This is a gift of God not a sacrament nor a substitute for a sacrament. It can be a dynamic response to and release of all you have known in Baptism and Confirmation. You cannot earn it, nor do you deserve it, but you should follow certain guidelines to experience it according to the Scripture. John 1:33.

HAVE YOU A PERSONAL RELATIONSHIP WITH JESUS?

To experience the baptism you need first to make sure that you have accepted Jesus as your personal Savior and have been born again. The baptism of the Holy Spirit is only given to the believer. It is a separate experience from water baptism. "John baptized with water, but within a few days you will be baptized with the Holy Spirit." (Acts 1:15) In the first we experience a *Presence* - in the second a full release of *POWER* as we are immersed in God's Spirit.

BE SURE THERE IS NO UNCONFESSED SIN IN YOUR LIFE

If there is someone whom you have not forgiven, or if you are aware of bitterness, hatred or resentment in your heart, make your peace with God and man.

TAKE AUTHORITY OVER DEMONIC CONTROL

"LORD show me and take from my life anything that is rooted in the satanic-books, records, tapes, jewelry, artifacts, etc. I renounce these in the name of Jesus."

ASK JESUS TO FULLY RELEASE WITHIN YOU THE POWER OF HIS HOLY SPIRIT - TO BAPTIZE YOU IN THE HOLY SPIRIT

Put away all fears. "For God has not given us the spirit of fear, but of power, love and a sound mind" (I Timothy 1:7). Sometimes it is more effective to have a group of Spirit baptized Christians pray with you. However, if you don't know of such a group, don't let this hinder you from praying the following prayer.

A PRAYER FOR EXPERIENCING THE BAPTISM

Dear Jesus, Your Word says in Revelation 3:20, "Behold I stand at the door and knock, if anyone hears my voice and opens the door I will come in . . ." Jesus, I open the door of my heart. Come in and be my personal Savior. Thank You for keeping Your Word.

Jesus I am sorry for all the times that I have sinned. Forgive me, take away all my bitterness, my hatred and my resentment. I forgive_____ (name those you need to forgive) even as you have forgiven me.

I renounce Satan and all his work and all the kingdoms of darkness. I renounce any power in me that is not under the Lordship of Jesus Christ. I renounce despair, discouragement and seeing myself as worthless. I take you Jesus as my Lord and Savior, my deliverer from all evil and my healer from all sickness and the scars of my past life. I accept myself as mightily loved by God the Father. I accept myself as powerfully saved by God the Son. I accept the Holy Spirit as promised of the Father, as my Counselor, my Comforter, my Teacher, and my pledge of the Kingdom of love forever.

Jesus, baptize me now in Your Holy Spirit. Fully release within me all the power, all the gifts, and all the fruit of Your Holy Spirit. Release within me a new power to praise You both in English and in tongues. As a response of faith I will now praise You in my new prayer language . . . In Jesus' Name, Amen.

AFTER THE BAPTISM OF THE HOLY SPIRIT

Realize the purpose of this new relationship with God: His Spirit is forming Christ's life in you so that you may accomplish the Father's will (Luke 1:35; Eph. 1:13-14).

Rejoice in the Trinity: the companionship of the Holy Spirit, union with Jesus, and the loving care of our Father. One should never feel alone after receiving the Baptism in the Holy Spirit. Realize that God enjoys your companionship and wants you to enjoy His (2 Cor. 1:20-22).

Don't worry about: (a) what to do; the Holy Spirit's wisdom is available to you (1 Cor. 2:6-13); (b) how to do it; the Holy Spirit's power is available to you (Luke 23:49); (c) what to say; the Holy Spirit will teach you (Luke 12:11-12); (d) what you are; be patient with your faults and failings. Cooperate patiently with the Holy Spirit's work of sanctification in you (2 Peter 1:3-11).

Rededicate yourself to your vocation in life; re-examine your responsibilities, your relationships to your family, church, community, co-workers. Express your love of God in service of others (Matt. 25:31-46).

Keep yourself free to recognize and respond to the promptings of the Holy Spirit. This means casting out fear and inhibition (2 Tim. 1:7). Pray for discernment of spirits. Seek guidance when it is available.

Be ready to witness to the Good News when the occasion is offered. Speak of God's goodness to you (John 9:1-38) and the reason why you believe in His promise.

Try to pray always, thanking God for His goodness to you and simply and joyfully praising that infinite goodness. Pray for your needs, those of the community, the Church, all mankind. You have an efficacious power in prayer now; you have only to use it confidently (Eph. 6:18). Adapt your prayer to your attractions and circumstances. The psalms will help you to praise God. Keep your prayer life simple and spontaneous.

Realize the importance of spending some time alone with God each day. Christ often went aside to pray alone (Matt. 14:23; Luke 6:12).

Read Scripture often (2 Tim. 3:14-17; 2 Peter 1:16-21). This will strengthen your faith that God has fulfilled His promise to send you the Holy Spirit in all His Power. Read books that will nourish your prayer and lead you to a deeper knowledge of the wonderful works of God, especially through Jesus.

Be faithful to your chosen prayer group. Christ makes Himself known most clearly through the Holy Spirit's action within a body of believers. Be assured that you will grow in the life of the Holy Spirit within the community of believers in which you embarked upon a life of faith and confidence in the power of the Holy Spirit. (I am in the midst of you, Romans 8:14-30).

READERS' COMMENTS

"A powerful witness and very valuable for Christian unity." *Fr. Fred Buckley, In radio ministry, Tampa Fla.*

"After reading your book, I send you the same invitation Paul gave: 'Come to Macedonia and help us !' " *Aristotle Kariyikades, FGBM Greece*

"Wow, God! is simple, powerful, exciting, hard to put down and will profoundly touch its readers. May they be legion." *Fr. Armond Nigro, S.J., Director of Retreats, Gonzaga University, Spokane, Wash.*

"I felt like I was in a Holy Ghost shower all the while I was reading." *John Fritz Fredrickson, College student studying for the Lutheran ministry.*

"What a bridge your book has been! As I've been able to witness to Catholic and non-Catholic friends your book has been an open door." *Delores Mix, A housewife*

"I think that you have fired the shot that will be heard around the world." *Sister Margaret Mangrich, A Milwaukee School Sister of Notre Dame*

"The chapter on 'tongues' was the best I have read anywhere on the subject as being informative and convincing, yet unemotional and practical." *Msgr. Francis Friedl, Former President of Loras College, Dubuque, IA*

From China: "A friend received your book from an American friend who passed it on to me. I was so deeply moved that I would like my own copy to further study how to attain the joy, peace, and contentment you have written in your book." *Teresa Lee, Malaysia, China*

About the Author

Sister Francis Clare, S.S.N.D. author, speaker, teacher, counselor, has been in full time service to the Charismatic Renewal for fourteen years. With roots in Iowa, sister presently lives with a Charismatic community of School Sisters of Notre Dame in West Allis, Wisconsin. She travels internationally giving days of renewal, retreats, and parish missions. Above every other gift sister's ministry is to stir up the gifts within you. Her home base is Saint Rita's Convent, 6023 West Lincoln, West Allis, Wisconsin 53219.